This book is dedicated to all who care deeply enough
to work to protect and nurture the planet we depend on.

CLIMATE
SENSE

A Practical Guide to Finding Solutions
and Keeping Your Cool

Patricia Hinkley

Visit our website at **www.StillwaterPress.com** for more information.

First Stillwater River Publications Edition

Library of Congress Control Number: 2018952138

ISBN-10: 1-946-30071-3
ISBN-13: 978-1-946-30071-3

1 2 3 4 5 6 7 8 9 10
Written by Patricia Hinkley
Cover art by Patricia Hinkley
Published by Stillwater River Publications, Pawtucket, RI, USA.

>Publisher's Cataloging-In-Publication Data
>(Prepared by The Donohue Group, Inc.)
>
>Names: Hinkley, Patricia.
>Title: Climate sense : a practical guide to finding solutions and keeping your cool /
>   Patricia Hinkley.
>Description: First Stillwater River Publications edition. | Pawtucket, RI, USA :
>   Stillwater River Publications, [2018]
>Identifiers: ISBN 9781946300713 | ISBN 1946300713
>Subjects: LCSH: Climate change mitigation. | Energy conservation. | Renewable
>   energy sources. | Waste minimization. | Sustainable living.
>Classification: LCC TD171.75 .H56 2018 | DDC 363.738746--dc23

Patricia Hinkley's love for the world and faith in humanity is evident on every page of her book. This book is at once a thorough, sobering dive into the implications of climate change, and a hopeful reminder of our potential for transformative change and altruistic cooperation. The reader is invited to explore and absorb devastating climate news while learning practices to process the information and move forward with action. This practical book will be an excellent companion for anyone wondering "what can I do!?" about climate change.

—Marina Mails
Climate Coach and Counselor

This book gets people to address some very deep emotional/grieving issues in a way that encourages action, not exasperation. The actionable items list is great and well organized. The balance of bad news and good/inspiration is good.

—J. Timmons Roberts
Professor of Environmental Studies
Brown University

A clarion call for collaborative climate action. Hinkley argues convincingly that the time for passively waiting for someone else to "fix" climate change is long over. The only way to win the climate change war is for each of us to choose a weapon, no matter how small. Collectively, we can and must shift the climate change conversation from despair to hope, from apathy to action. This book is a good place to start.

—Joan Sullivan
Renewable Energy Photographer

Anecdotal stories make Climate Sense a delight to read, giving a personal touch to an informative description of the critical environmental issues of our time. Anyone who has felt overwhelmed by the looming threat to our existence can take inspiration from the author's attempts to do her part to reduce her carbon footprint and to encourage others to do so. One walks away with a broader understanding of the issues, and renewed resolve to join with others in tackling the climactic problems facing our beautiful blue-green planet earth.

—Carol Khalsa

Pat Hinkley's ability to connect with easy to read layperson language changes incomprehensible scientific jargon into comprehensible ideas which inspired me to want to do my part to help. Her fictionalized short stories and her awesome action steps showed me how I can do just that.

A gentle encouragement for the reader to stop and breathe when overwhelm sets in set the tone of the entire book for me. While there is much negativity surrounding the fact of climate change, Hinkley chooses to focus on the positive—the power of uniting many people—each one making one small change at a time. She excels at illustrating how every individual can make a choice to help effect a reversal on the cataclysmic chain of events set in place by mankind's overuse of our planet's resources.

—Bonita Osley
Writer

Also by Patricia Hinkley

Claiming Space:
Finding Stillness that Inspires Action

————————

Chasing Sleep:
Lonely Tussles in the Dark

gratitude

Gratitude fills me for kind friends who moved this project forward.

Bonita Osley graciously read, edited and shared her perspectives to help bring the book into being.

The eagle eyes of Edie Stahlberger and Stillwater River Publishing saw the seemingly impossible edits waiting yet to be seen.

Carol Khalsa read and shared her climate-informed perspective. Joanne Walsh lent her scientific eye to the reading.

My daughter, Sarai Hinkley gave the book her support and reality checking.

Thank you all!

CONTENTS

PREFACE

This is a book I finally had to write. The thoughts provoking the writing have rumbled around my head for years. I am a veteran of the gas lines in the 1970's, when many of us mothers with young children packed breakfasts for the morning rituals of waiting to buy gas. My two children nibbled on Cheerios and sipped chocolate milk in the car while we lingered an hour for our turn at the pump.

Something certainly seemed wrong way back then. This interruption in gas supplies was about an embargo of oil by the Organization of the Petroleum Exporting Countries (OPEC); yet its blatant message gave pause to look at our oil-dependent lifestyles. However, after a while and after the embargo ended, abundant gasoline returned and we went on with our lives.

Computer projections from the 1970's confirmed the sense of something out of kilter when Donnella Meadows[1] and her team of computer scientists presented their predictions for a climate growing out of balance—forecasts which since the 70's have mostly borne out, except for two details:

Computers could not predict the cascading events of nature adjusting to major stressors—as when coral reefs became distressed, and many fish species lost dependable reef habitats and nurseries. Each progression, or feedback loop, intensifies and

[1] Donella Meadows, Jorgen Randers, and Dennis Meadows, *The Limits to Growth* (Vermont: Chelsea Green Publishing, 2004)

speeds up negative changes and challenges the earth's natural ability to recover.

The political climate has been contradictory at best. President Carter listened to scientific proposals, and told the public about the inherent dangers of climate change. He urged lowering thermostats and putting on warmer clothes rather than raising the house temperature. Carter illustrated the gravity of the situation and placed solar panels on the White House. He called for installing enough solar panels in the U.S. to decrease fossil fuel emissions by 20% in 2020.

Forty-eight years is a long thinking process about the meaning for us all when the climate changes radically. Carter's good advice was mocked by pseudo-wise pundits, and the next president, Ronald Reagan, removed the solar panels. Many people turned away from disturbing forecasts they did not want to hear. For decades, much as Cassandra of Greek mythology uttered true prophecies no one believed, modern day prophets despair at the worsening course of climate events. And here we are now, still turning away and debating in 2018.

You may not believe in climate change; nonetheless, I urge you to consider that climate change is no longer a matter of belief; we are well beyond this discussion. Look around and educate yourself about the strangely devastating events we are witnessing.

There are many ways to amend our contributions to climate change. Advanced means are being devised to attract attention to how far down the path of danger we have come. In fact, a major mobilization is being called for; something on the scale of the

World War II efforts where everyone joined in with their small or large contributions. Teaming up in a steadfast effort to solve challenges became a patriotic duty. Perhaps the summer of severe storms in 2017 plus the droughts, floods and fires in 2018 will waken us to what I consider *THE* most important story trying to get our attention, mostly, but not always, behind the scenes— until now.

Climate change is an existential crisis
threatening the very existence of our way of life, if not life itself.

My writing began a week before undisputed trauma struck the U.S. mainland and the Caribbean islands. On August 17, 2017, Category 4 Hurricane Harvey struck Houston and its surrounding areas. Two weeks of torrential rains dropped 40-52" of water onto neighborhoods, business areas and nearby towns. Compromised oil refineries along the Texas coastline compounded the disaster by spewing dangerous petrochemicals into the waters that inundated communities. The level of calamity following the hurricane, coupled with this amount of water falling from the lingering clouds, challenged our comprehension. But then, more storms were brewing off the coast of western Africa.

In the cataclysmic summer of hurricanes, an earthquake struck southern Mexico. Then Irma roared in as a Category 5 hurricane, devastating Caribbean islands before it darted from one place of destruction to another in the long state of Florida. Seven million people created the largest mass evacuation in recent memory. The only highway on the Florida Keys was severed and houses lost electricity. Many residents could not return to their homes for months.

As if these disasters weren't enough, the weaker Hurricane Jose came along with enough vigor to keep jittery people on edge. Maria followed quickly on Jose's heels as a Category 5 hurricane to pummel islands in the Caribbean already mercilessly trounced. Then Maria devastated Puerto Rico so badly its electrical system has so far taken over *a year* to repair many, but not all, of the power outages. This is serious; a substantial island in the Caribbean Sea was totally cut off from life-sustaining power, clean water, medical and other supplies. The Virgin Islands and others also lie shattered in their enticing aqua waters and once pristine beaches. Sadly, the United States government, rather than help, sat waiting while island people's medications ran out and mold grew on walls and ceilings. Residents developed illnesses from the mold. Citizens in this territory of the United States, who had lived with air conditioning and modern conveniences, were thrust backward into primitive living.

In case anyone was becoming complacent in the fast-paced news cycle of summer 2017, a 7.1 magnitude earthquake struck near Mexico City, cause horrendous damage in the city. Three hundred and seventy people died and much of the city lies in ruin.

Without time to catch a breath, another hurricane swept across the extra-warm waters of the Gulf of Mexico, building steam and heading for the coastlines of Alabama, Mississippi and Florida. Even though every on-edge person was alarmed, fortunately Hurricane Nate was small and not as damaging. The season was far from over, however. A small, late October storm with 70-80 mile per hour winds traveled up the eastern coast of the U.S. to leave 1.2 million people in the Northeast without power, especially in New England.

All these happenings give me great respect for the power of nature, especially when it runs amuck. Some say these storms are a forecast of what is to come. Certainly they are highly unusual and scary. They carry more water, linger longer, and stretch vast distances. Category 4 and 5 hurricanes are known statistically as one in 100- or 500-year events. There's a good description of 1 in 500-year storms in Vox.[2] These storms have a 1% or 5% chance of happening within these time frames. Hurricanes Irma and Marie are destroying the odds, though, for they happened within a two-week span. This is bizarre and highly abnormal.

[2] Dara Lind, "The '500-year' Flood, Explained: Why Houston was so Underprepared for Hurricane Harvey," *Vox Magazine*, August 28, 2017.

CHAPTER 1
Introduction

A long habit of not thinking a thing wrong,
gives it a superficial appearance of being right,
and raises at first a formidable outcry in defense of custom.
But the tumult soon subsides.
Time makes more converts than reason.
—Thomas Paine

Common Sense by Thomas Paine advocated independence from Great Britain to people in the Thirteen Colonies. His pamphlets helped transform a colonial hornet's nest of citizens and leaders into the American Revolution.

Two hundred and forty-two years later we need a revolution in our thinking and conversations, so we, as a populace, can rise above the current squabbles about climate change. What does revolution in our thinking imply? Revolution, in terms of what I mean, is helped out in part by Merriam Webster's definition of a "fundamental change in the way of thinking about or visualizing something." An overriding new paradigm is called for in our attitudes toward what is happening in relation to our world. The thought processes for many people have been swayed by a resistant line of reasoning which does not want to conceive of or even allow the words "climate change" into the vocabulary. This detail is a stumbling block in light of the many who have been affected by the climate reordering. Climate change is self-evident to them.

We humans are equipped with an innate ability to use our common sense, a gift often easily sidetracked by louder voices seeking to convince us of our so-called wrongheadedness. *Climate Sense: A Practical Guide to Finding Solutions and Keeping Your Cool,* whose first tentative subtitle was called *How Not to Freak Out About the Changing Climate,* invites your inherent ability for sensible judgment to rise above the herd of opinions. I do write from a perspective of belief, since the 1970's, in the computer projections that showed exactly the progression we are experiencing, yet not as quickly as events unfold today. Ignoring risks which upset or reduce an essential, stable climate endangers us all. This book advocates for your independence from opinions which stray from proven science. Your common sense is a vital attribute which is imperative to call on right now to clear our minds on the climate issue—to seek *climate sense* amongst the conflicting stories.

Observation is fundamental to this sensible way of thinking—and I don't mean looking at a snowball packed tight and brought inside to the Senate floor, as Senator Inofe did to demonstrate the cold weather in winter. I refer to your personal discernment, along with climate science reports from monitoring and scrutiny beyond what our eyes and ears are able to perceive. When you put together observation and intellect, you will see 97% of career climate scientists concurring with the huge amounts of data amassed about forecasts, past history and trends from extremely accurate projections since the 1980's. These trends are well documented to show human influence over decades of obser-vation.[3,4] Time is quickly revealing the truthfulness of their surveillance and models. The only exceptions are the accelerated consequences beyond their factoring. It is reasonable to allow *some* results of their expertise into our decision-making.

A 97% agreement amongst scientists is a staggering number. Even so, I acknowledge the thoughts of others who see things differently. Some people see these changes as natural cyclical occurrences—weather, in fact. Some people believe less trust-worthy sources of information and discount the information from those who have dedicated their lives to studying climate science. Bob (pseudonym) is a very intelligent, well-read, and articulate representative for these counterpoints. He sees human inter-ference as a dot on the whole timespan of vast geologic and huge alterations throughout earth's history—and there is nothing to do. Bob blames corporations for their part in accelerating change. This cynical approach troubles me; for time spent blaming and chasing after corporations wastes precious moments needed for

---

[3] Union of Concerned Scientists. UCCS.org. climate.nasa.gov/causes, carbonbrief.org/analysis-why-scientists-think-100-of-global-warming-is-human-caused. European Environmental Agency. eea.europa.eu/.../climate/.../how-do-human-activities-contribute-to-climate-change.
[4]*Recurrence Intervals and 100-Year Floods* – US Geological Survey. https://water.usgs.gov/edu/100yearflood.html.

more constructive response. I don't want to go there while time for acting is still at hand.

Does it make sense to ignore rising waters pouring under your doorstep or to ignore increasingly vicious storms happening more frequently? If you knew a big storm was coming, wouldn't you want to prevent or at least protect what you could? If you saw a truck veering toward you, wouldn't you quickly jump out of the way? I can't sit around doing nothing while the stability we depend upon deteriorates.

A one-in-five-hundred-year chance of happening in any year is a rare event. Getting back to the topic of observation, common sense says, "Wow, look at these 100- and 500-year[5] storms now happening every three years or every two weeks. Wow, look at how vast the storms are." Even the small Hurricane Jose rumbled up the East Coast of the United States and lingered as a tropical storm, with high winds and heavy seas strong enough to keep Rhode Island fishermen ashore for four days. Jose was not a damaging hurricane as Category 4 Harvey and Maria were, yet Jose's length of time circling offshore was uncommon. Two hurricanes of such intensity never before pounded the United States in one season, let alone within weeks of each other. Never had one hurricane spent three days as a Category 5 in the open Atlantic. Storms extending across the entire eastern seaboard from Florida to Maine are new behavior. Gales and strong winds in the past could be severe, yet they were more localized. Now hurricanes affect millions of people across vast swaths of the

---

[5] *Recurrence Intervals and 100-Year Floods* – US Geological Survey. https://water.usgs.gov/edu/100yearflood.html.

country. Devastated cities, towns and islands lie in ruin after their passage. Hurricanes once upon a time swooped through, did their damage, weakened, and left. No more. Now they linger for days or even weeks while dropping tons and tons of water on the land and inhabitants below. Noticing these events is observation.

Look at the eroding beaches in Rhode Island[6] and at the flooded streets on a normal day in Miami Beach, where fish now swim alongside people wading to a coffee shop.[7,8] Look at the "sunny day floods"[9] in Norfolk, Virginia, Wilmington, Delaware, and the North and South Carolina coastlines, to name a few. Search Google for "sunny day floods" to learn more because these events don't often make the news, even though they matter to the people who live there. The fact of their happening matters to us all, for they are signs and signals to heed.

A move away from the coastlines shows historic flooding in the Midwest. Deluges raining down. Look at the plentiful, very strong, and costly tornados ripping across the midwestern tornado alley from Iowa to Texas, and recently across a more southerly "Dixie Alley" from Louisiana to Georgia.[10] Look at the historic amounts of snow in the 2016 northeastern winter. Remember the mountain-high piles of dirty white plowed-up snow with nowhere

[6] *Losing Ground,* RI Coastal Resources Management Council, 2012.
[7] Eileen Mignoni, "Flooding is the New Normal in Miami," *Yale Climate Connections,* February 6, 2017.
[8] "Encroaching Tides in Miami-Dade County, Florida," *Union of Concerned Scientists* magazine fact sheet, 2016.
[9] Jonathan Corum, "A Sharp Increase In 'Sunny Day' Flooding," *The New York Times,* September 3, 2016.
[10] Daniel Levitt, "With Increased Destruction, a New Tornado Alley Emerges," *Bloomberg,* August 18, 2017.

else for it to go at the so-called Boston snow farm? Have you noticed challenges now to flying across the country, in winter, in tornado season—whenever—depending on the country-wide disruptions to airports made by storms on that day? Look at the unusually high winds and now commonplace windier conditions in many places. Strong winds now seem to be the normal in my area. Feel the increased humidity and temperatures. Look at the mold growing inside and outside your house. Do you notice more insects eating the vegetables you grow? Those damnable little white moths continued all summer long to hatch kale-eating caterpillars. Do you see trees distressed with their leaves eaten by gypsy moths or by pine bark beetles or borers of some kind? Do you see more brown trees on the hillsides, waiting for the all-too-frequent forest fires?

I ask your patience and forbearance in reading *Climate Sense,* that you hold your mind open to what affects us now and will greatly affect future generations. You may not agree with the 97% of scientific concurrence, but something out of the ordinary is truly happening most everywhere and in the events stretching beyond many of our historical memories. Yes, storms are worse in some years than others, temperatures fluctuate lower and higher; however, the scope and frequency of storms has changed. There appears to be no standard anymore. Hold your nose if this possibility is so distasteful to comprehend, and look around you. What do you see? Has normal changed recently in your area? What does your sound judgement tell you beyond the sensationalist, political or denialist news? Holding misgivings about anything helps you come to a conclusion. It's good to question; perhaps though, you may want to weigh those doubts with what you observe as you cast your net of inquiry broadly. Call on your very own common sense. When you look around and really take it in, the conversation begins. There is much we can do when we accept the reality of the reordering going on.

Look at the intense heat in the southwest and the western parts of the U.S. One hundred and six degrees in always chilly San Francisco?[11] Look at the immense, fierce and far-flung scenes of entire mountains on fire—portraying apocalyptic scenes across the west. Ask the thousands who have fled or lost their homes. Ask the flooded-out people of Houston or the residents of Puerto Rico still living without electricity months after the hurricane passed through.

Good sense says no—this does not feel normal. Even if you live in a peaceful, delightfully unaffected region, lucky you; nonetheless, it does not feel commonplace for hosts of others. Normal has shifted.

Take a look at the dislocated people across the world. Thirty-two districts in Bangladesh have been under water, affecting 8 million people after flooding.[12] This is a faraway land which is unimaginable to many of us in the U.S.; nevertheless, Bangladeshi people are now on the move, seeking asylum and new homes. As islands in Micronesia in the Pacific Ocean disappear beneath the rising

---

[11] Steve Rubenstein, Nanette Asimov, and Jenna Lyons, "San Francisco Hits 106 Degrees—Shatters All-Time Record," *SF Gate*, September 2, 2017.
[12] *Bangladesh: Floods and Landslides.* ReliefWeb.int June 2017.

seas,[13] their displaced residents must relocate. Drought scorches away farmlands in Africa where photographs now reveal increasingly vast arid plains of empty lands.[14] These Africans are leaving their ancestral homes because nothing grows on these lands and consequently they can no longer feed their families. Drought also affects much of Mexico,[15] whose people would like to be on the move to more habitable climes. Puerto Ricans, with no way to earn a living or pay for food and family needs, will not remain on the island. They too will migrate elsewhere. All of these people on the move are climate refugees.

A mass migration of displaced persons ripples out everywhere they move. Most countries are willing to absorb some climate refugees—up to a point, while striving to retain their unique cultural significance. Yet each country has a stopping point for the numbers of foreign-born people they are willing to absorb. When doors close, where do homeless beings go? Look at the strife already brought about by too many Syrian, Eritrean and Afghan migrants flowing into Europe and seeking strained resources to feed their families.[16]

Look at the conditions in the coldest places on earth where glaciers and icebergs are retreating and then vanishing. What does being diluted by huge quantities of fresh water mean for the oceans, or for the many species of saltwater animals whose lives

---

[13] Alice Klein, "Eight Low-lying Pacific Islands Swallowed Whole by Rising Seas," *New Scientist*, September 7, 2017.

[14] *A climate in crisis*. Oxfam.org. April 27, 2017.

[15] Noe Torres, "Mexican Farmers Suffer Worst Drought in 70 Years," Reuters.com. November 25, 2011.

[16] *Mapped: How the Migration crisis is a Strain on Europe's Democracies*. Raziye Akkoc. 1/21/16. The Telegraph.

depend on a consistent supply of that water? How is the earth's balance affected when tons and tons of polar ice melt and its iciness disperses into the oceans?

Now is the moment to allow the questions to fully sink into your awareness. This book will delve deeper into detail and look at solutions later. For now though it is enough to simply question and absorb what you observe personally or by way of television and radio. I'm noticing how bizarre it is to see pink azaleas and forsythia blossoming along the walkways on a December morning dog walk in Rhode Island, where most years the ground would be frozen and the air would be freezing. Global weirding indeed.

Perhaps you will take a big overview of climate-related events happening all around you. It may be you will try to make sense of changes both near to you and in those altering faraway places, in ways which will affect us all eventually. No one is immune. The scale of the changing planet is indeed daunting. Your commonsensical responses matter so much, for they help you and all of us respect this shared truth. Then we can do what is possible to limit worsening conditions, to protect ourselves and to plan for the consequences. A positive approach to what is so overwhelming keeps each of us from simply waiting for whatever is to come our way. We become actors rather than victims of the climate vicissitudes.

Acknowledging the sense embodied in your resistance to such daunting thoughts is important. Certainly no singular Texas or Florida hurricane, Kansas or Alabama tornado, California or Montana wildfire, a tropical disease or crop failure abroad is solely about climate change. You're right there. However, the overall effect of the planet warming shows up in rapidly cascading events happening one upon the other. The risks for more frequent and intense storms increase then, as does uncertainty for us all. Where and when will who-knows-what disaster strike next? A practical approach is crucial, vital, and imperative to make use of right now. *Climate Sense* argues for stepping off the curb of by-standing while you wait for a leader to take charge. The book calls on us all to open our eyes and ears and hearts to fully comprehend the nature of what nature is doing.

Making the state of the climate real for yourself may compel you to act as if all of what is transpiring over the world matters. It really does matter. When this becomes real to you, the power of your individual choices and actions replaces a sense of powerlessness pinning you like a butterfly to a board. Do you want to be stuck in hopelessness when you could be flying with a renewed respect for nature, agriculture, water and air? We will all benefit from your renewal.

You've just read a heavy dose of the terrible—now it's time to look at positive messages from encouraging projects. The intention of weaving between supportive thoughts, doses of bad news, strategies to do now, and imaginary little stories of differing groups of people—is to call on and inspire your highest and best self toward the collective benefit of the whole world.

Aspirational, right?

Finding good news, even when it's daunting to spot in the midst of so much chatter, props up our sanity. The movie "Prosperity,"[17] released in 2017, is a helpful dose of encouraging accomplishments by people thinking ahead and acting upon challenges. This film shows people and companies doing good for others and for the world while profiting at the same time. It dismisses the idea that doing right by the world means you make no money. One effect needn't rule out the other. Positive messages are not meant to sugarcoat the climate horrors, which are in fact frightful. Huge frequent catastrophes and unrelenting bad news lead me to crave a breath of fresh air filled with other perspectives which bring to light new points of view and solutions.

The challenges of the changing climate are beyond what a single individual mind clinging to old ways of thinking can figure out. However, receptive minds joined together create a collective intelligence much greater than one lone thinker. We human beings can take a hint from how computers link together in creating the artificial intelligence known as AI. Perhaps our linked minds will coalesce into an enhanced human intelligence vast enough to guide us, and for all one knows, with the assistance of AI. We need all the help we can find.

Despite beginning with the gravity of the bad news, *Climate Sense* is truthfully an optimistic declaration to be part of a "moonshot" approach to an immense game of inspiring and transforming

---

[17] "Prosperity," an informational/motivational series. https://www.well.org

human lethargy into working together to sustain our world. The goal is lofty—to wake up and join forces and to make great changes in how we live.

What follows next begins the interludes between chapters—five stories about different ages of people talking with each other about their reactions to and what they will do about climate change. Instead of turning away—turn toward these possibilities as you read on.

Never underestimate the power of one person taking a stand.
The power of one begins
when one person changes her mind from "I can't" to
"what can I do?"
This is profound internal power!

Friends Joining Together
A Story

A group of long-time companions are talking at their favorite coffee shop. Laughter bubbles up easily as they share their foibles in learning to live more lightly. Each friend has come to understand how climate change isn't going away and because of this certainty, every one of them wants to and needs to live their lives more simply. Being in harmony with the earth is the new way for this group of millennials who truly understand the quandary of the age into which they were born. So they help each other figure out best ways to manage the challenges.

Susie excitedly begins the conversation. "My new job is so great, especially after leaving that company selling third-world-manufactured clothes produced by seamstresses earning lowest level wages. Now I help people become fit and healthy by teaching them the body mechanics of working outside. I am happy because it feels good to be doing something positive in the world!"

Everyone howls at the image of teaching people fitness by working outside rather than going to gyms, but Susie continues,

"No, really, they love it. I'm teaching them basic skills, how not to hurt themselves and to feel invigorated in the process. I teach them to rake leaves and bend their knees when they move firewood. Good stuff for us all to learn these days, because we may need to take care of things more on our own. It's important to stay strong, and what better way to do it than with outside work. It feels good, you get to listen to the birds and feel the wind on your face. My students are learning to work together as a team, in a pace similar to how farmers work. They take breaks, laugh, talk, and then feeling refreshed, get back to working with their plants. These overall healthy approaches to working are something most of us have forgotten about or never even learned. My students will be stronger and more resilient with whatever climate change throws at us."

Mary chimes in, "Well, I just quit my unsatisfying job to begin making healthy foods for people, and I love it," she glows.

Andrea, who left a brokerage firm in New York, says, "At least I have a cushion for a while so I can sort out what I'd really like to do. I just couldn't keep on putting my head in the sand about the climate changes and how we personally and our companies contribute to making it worse. It's just not right for some of us and our companies to degrade the planet for generations to come. This so-called "free market" is not free at all, and I no longer want to be involved with it. I want to be part of the great changes people are creating. I'm excited by the positive stuff going on that I read about! In the meanwhile, I am enjoying life, being outside, and learning more about myself."

"That's so cool, Andrea," affirms Susie. "Good for you!"

Andrea continues, thinking out loud. "It could just be, I want to tell others what we are doing and why it is important and also… to let them know that changing is not so hard. We here are doing it, after all—so how bad can it be? I think I want to make this conversation familiar to lots of people."

"That could be a really good thought, Andrea," Mary answers. "You are good at communicating and what you have done in leaving a cushy job takes courage and commitment. You are passionate about standing for the earth! Yea for you."

Annie pipes up with her new idea. "Why don't we make a game of it? Let's tell each other what we have switched out for more long-lasting, healthier, or more local ways? And let's do one thing—answer each other with, '*yes, and*…' instead of 'yeah, I hear you, *but*…' The word BUT is a big stopper to whatever is just said. Language makes such a difference in how we allow or close off new ideas. I want to welcome all suggestions."

"Oh, those are good thoughts," says Mary as she mimics '*and*' … "just today I found a solar generator. It's quiet, not like those ugly roaring gas-powered ones, which during a recent power outage sounded like being in hell. Not that I know what hell is like, of course," smiles all around, "but what I imagine hell would include. Anyway, it's a reliable generator that gets its power from the sun and keeps things going in my house. Plus, buying it supports people doing good in the world."

"This is what I mean," says Annie. "We bring ideas to each other and challenge ourselves to step up more. Together we can do this and maybe others will notice. Perhaps other people will join us in sustaining the quality of lives for generations to come. I certainly don't want my answer to be 'nothing' when my children ask what I was doing in the early 2000's when we all knew climate change was nipping at our heels."

CHAPTER 2
The Dilemma

The basic physics of the climate are well understood.
Burning fossil fuels emits carbon dioxide.
And carbon dioxide is a greenhouse gas
which traps heat in the atmosphere.
There is no debate about that.
The link is as certain as the link between smoking and cancer.

—Christine Todd Whitman
Former Environmental Protection Agency administrator

A debate rages about the terms 'weather' versus 'climate.' Notwithstanding, there is more to the discussion, for observation over time tells a more comprehensive story than the simple name called weather can possibly convey. The arguments between the two words also focus on sensible matters of assessing human influence as well as the costs of making changes. A debate that informs us about all parts of a very complex subject is a healthy process to learning what is feasible and then to moving forward. The war of words, however, is not the stopping point.

Weather alone is specific to current atmospheric conditions in a certain area. The snow which Senator Inofe brought as a snowball to the Senate in 2015 was part of a great snowfall in one particular place. It was freakin' cold and there was too much snow. This flaky event is called weather and does not indicate widespread cold spanning over a long time period. Climate, conversely, refers to weather conditions prevailing in general over lengthy durations. The difference has to do with time: weather is immediate, climate is long-term.

The political climate is a whole other issue. Senator Inofe is but one example of the politicians who want to believe climate change is not real. They may receive their information from partisan news sources or they may be motivated by wealthy constituents or by fossil fuel entities contributing enormous amounts of money to their re-election coffers. However they have formed their opinions, U.S. leaders such as this senator who deny the existence of climate change are putting their political futures before the welfare of the entire planet. Nonetheless, no matter the source, this one-sided information is not sufficient when 97% of climate scientists across the world agree that climate change is a real and crucial issue.

We citizens deserve political representatives
who do their research into unbiased sources,
because misguided information ultimately hurts us all.

Stories from all parts of the world support the need for truth telling about the climate changes. Amidar Ghosh is a Bangladeshi author who is up to date with the catastrophic results on exceedingly populated areas experiencing climate change. He has a wide-ranging perspective seldom understood by Americans. He talks about "humanity's great derangement,"[18] wording which well defines our all-too-human inability to perceive the scale of the looming catastrophe. This is a very strange kind of instability indeed, where our refusal to see the havoc brewing on the horizon affects the whole planet. Climate changes hidden to many Americans are speeding up and intensifying. The time has come for stepping away from this derangement so we can move forward.

Inestimable amounts of money hide behind the denial of global warming. Specifically, Charles and David Koch and the Robert Mercer family fund much of the biased climate information campaigns. In 2011, the Political Economy Research Institute at the University of Massachusetts reported that "Koch Industries and its subsidiaries emitted over twenty-four *million* tons of carbon dioxide from fifty sites." Talk about substantial emissions ...and these releases continue even as the Koch brothers rail on with years of concerted financial backing for lobbying and even more maliciously, for educating people to their one-sided and dangerously limited viewpoint. Great numbers of congressional leaders receive funding from and are beholden especially to these two families and others who refuse to acknowledge the validity and the science of climate change. The "great derangement" has

---

[18] Ghosh, Amitav. The Great Derangement. Climate Change and the Unthinkable. University of Chicago Press. 2016

been arranged and is not and never was beneficial, especially now when time grows short for turning the momentum. This campaign, however, has been exceedingly profitable.

Fortunately, deniers do not have the only voices in the room. In reality, their loud opinions represent a tiny segment of the global population. Unfortunately the debates have sown confusion in many minds and gotten in the way of people's looking to what they can do. A relatively hidden majority of people know climate change is real and concur about our ability to reduce the effects. They look for empowering ideas to tackle and awaken from their reticence.

Climate Sense is not only for those people who still doubt the reality of a changing climate (if this applies, please read on anyway.) More significantly though, I write for people who understand the issue and still fail to grasp the speed with which the world is reordering itself. Many of us say, yes, I know climate change is happening—and then go on about our business. The climate is changing so fast that each of us must take action in response. This book is especially written to motivate you.

Even while the ordinary public waits for leadership, corporations who understand how climate change will negatively affect their bottom lines are springing to action. Money talks, so they ignore the loud resistant voices and move forward to instigate constructive adaptations in how they do business. Some states are grasping how a pro-active stance helps them and their residents. Together businesses and state and local governments are creating a groundswell of action. Their momentum is especially advantageous to countering the fatalistic attitude of numbers of young people who assume nothing can be done in time to stop the runaway train. The robust progress underway is an inspirational counterpoint to the mostly negative news stories filling the airwaves. Accounts of what we can do will get us off the dime, so to speak, and will motivate us all.

Climate change is a huge dilemma, it's true; still, I want to believe that as we mobilize and encourage more people to respond constructively, carbon emissions will dovetail their decreased emissions. Finding this impetus requires lots of us to pay attention and to make the changes asked of us. One person makes changes, as does another and another and so on.

Ultimately, we *need to* and will *want to* live more in harmony with a changing earth as a guidepost for what must be done.

Disputes about climate and weather also mask a deep underlying fear our minds fail to comprehend, of distressingly unfathomable transformations of life as usual. Major solutions are complicated, time consuming and costly; so, we ignore, deny, get busy and refuse to pay attention. Many Americans believe global warming is happening and carbon emissions should be lowered, but few think they will be affected personally. Even those who know the story turn away because for sure, we human beings are too intelligent for this. Someone else will deal with this later, we think…. someone will solve it.

Truthfully, the scale of climate change is scary and hard to conceive. It presents an existential fear of whether, in the worst predictions, we and our human species will continue to exist as is, or whether we will scrape by at all. This is unimaginable, oppressive, and provides a good reason to hide or to dispute the reality of this unthinkable magnitude. However, closed minds, no matter the reason, do not help anyone. And at this point, we need all the help we can get. You, me, and all of us.

While Chapter 7 examines the costs of action and inaction, let's first look at this very big fear which stops plenty of us. Denying the climate is even changing is confusing rhetoric which leads to a sense of impossibility about doing anything productive. Basic powerlessness takes away our capacity to act, saps our strength, depletes our resources, and leaves us feeling we lack the authority to act. By thinking we are out of ideas, we become at the mercy of what we cannot control. No one wants to feel powerless. Being victim to whatever climate throws at us is dismaying. Thus, we assume, if we don't look in that direction, it will all go away. But surprise, surprise, a changing climate won't go away.

What your explorations teach you may in truth reveal a climate quite different from what you have known. Strange events happening around you can give you a pause filled with moments to wonder what is going on. More investigation may be called for than the nightly news reports. Part of the reason we don't see much in the news about climate change is that huge and depressing news does not sell well. The other piece of the 'why' is a choice made by news organizations not to portray solutions. Nonetheless, it is time to listen to new points of view, to research and be open to your discovery. It is time to ask around and include your personal observations along with the reports from nearly 100% of people educated and trained in exquisitely monitoring climate in all parts of the planet. Paying attention, learning, being curious and deciding for yourself is as much as any of us can begin with. This is a momentous starting point. And if you choose not to do anything, opportunity always awaits a later change of mind.

New understandings lead us forward one step at a time. We don't get the whole answer all in a piece. Nonetheless, one basic overriding issue is that we human beings have overshot the earth's capacity to sustain ourselves. This means simply that the earth must replace what is used up. Such regeneration takes years of time to grow, time to replant, to reestablish and to husband as well as time for animals to mature. Great efforts are called on to repair damages and limit excessive carbon dioxide vapors in the atmosphere. The lateness of the hour dictates that we begin somewhere—as in now. The easiest place for most of us to start is by looking to how our own lives contribute to the problem.

Simply going down to the local hardware store is not an option for replacing new acres of farmlands or forests recently destroyed. The Ecological Footprint Network[19] (EFN), established to advance the science of sustainability, explains the overshooting process well. EFN measures both the demand on nature and the supply nature has available. There is a healthy balance of ecological

---

[19]EcologicalFootprintNetwork.org

assets needed by a population to provide for itself. In a nutshell, plant-based food and fiber products, livestock and fish, forest products and the space essential to urban infrastructure support our lives.

The earth's capacities to absorb and reuse waste and carbon emissions are huge issues. EFN concludes that if everyone on earth lives as we in the U.S. do, 4.1 planets will be required to sustain us all. Oops. What a conundrum. Humanity across the globe today requires 1.6 earths. Still oops, especially since this latter figure includes people in Burundi who live on $270 per year. The obvious issue is twofold: we only have one earth and few of us are willing to scale down to the standard with which Burundians live.

The crux of the remedy is: it is possible for many of us in the Western world to consume less, and to waste less than we habitually do. Developed countries have found very good, albeit short-sighted, responses to improving people's lives. The desirable end product of this progress, though, is a worrisome short-term aspect when nature has a very long-term approach. And guess what? Nature always wins.

A longer view is called for with respect to bringing our desires into better alignment with our true needs. Do we really *need* a new dress, or an extra special coffee maker, or a new muscle car? Do we need that latte every day? Many of us are not accustomed to comparing the actual meaning of the words want and need, and yet the moment is here to transform our thinking.

You can see how the debate is the first stumbling block. After you pick yourself up, the question then is, what do you do with what you learn? You may find yourself thinking, "First of all it's too big, and secondly I don't want to do anything about it. I can't see how what I do makes a difference anyway." Learning about climate change can overwhelm, discourage, and depress you into hopelessness, and who wants to go there? So with all this in mind, let's turn to some ways to positively balance yourself in the midst of these heavy looks at our future.

One suggestion is to give yourself some breathing space—
literal space between the words where you relax
and take a few breaths to center yourself.
Your job in this day of climate change is
to stop at the points of overwhelm,
and then to gently take a few breaths
as you remember the beauty and love in your life.
Thus, you expand your body, relax your mind
and interrupt the fear cycle of contraction.
Try it.

Trusting in the potential of your actions is another path forward. Small steps are best in most distressing situations. Gentle breathing and looking for beauty provide rest between the mighty currents of what you are learning. Coming to some sort of terms with climate change is a challenging balance beam to walk upon, and so all of us need to nourish ourselves into stronger stability. Balance and peacefulness are crucial.

Okay, so what do we do with the feelings brought up by the whole issue of a changing climate? Reading and re-reading this book is a strategy to keep your sanity and your footing, stable enough to be present sufficiently to hear beyond the bad news. Perhaps you will activate yourself around solutions. Then in becoming active, you become a beacon of light for other people wanting to be part of the solution as well. The real unknown quantity as far as climate change has to do with our behaviors—do we actually step out of old destructive patterns to embrace the possible? Do we wake up and change our habits, or will we be like a frog in a pot of water slowly coming to a climate boil?

Debate and then action leads to the third dimension of the puzzle. There is acceptance, education and action; then, time is of the essence. Humanity has puttered around the information about climate change for thirty years. *Thirty years*—and now time is not in our favor. Fossil fuel companies and apologists would have you believe climate change effects will be felt long hence, in the next century or not in your lifetime. They want you to believe that eventual solutions from someone or somewhere will save us. Yes, it is true technology is bringing us many answers—and rapidly, but these ways out of the dilemma only become viable when many of us take them up.

We people are the key piece to this trajectory.
A changing climate requires each of us to change our ways of life.

The degree of change called for depends on how soon people mobilize to mitigate processes already in motion. Carbon is spewing into the atmosphere every second. The more carbon infiltrates the air, the more ice melts and the more fires rage, the more carbon is released. Round and round it goes. Mobilizing early enough is tricky though. People need to know the extent of the dilemma without the hype which leads to fatalistic and static reactions. On the other hand, a realistic, optimistic and heartfelt approach encourages taking up worthwhile actions which successfully transition us to ways of living that do not depend on fossil fuels.

What gets in the way of acknowledging or doing anything about climate change is feeling powerless and unable to make a difference. Yet the truth is, each of us can and will significantly affect the overall progress. Constructive action springs us free of powerlessness and informs us that we are powerful indeed. Action also counteracts any niggling little hopeless thoughts trying to get a leg up on your choices.

The fourth issue then in coming to terms with climate change beyond debate, action and timing is your personal strategy of how you go about what you do. Begin with what is important to you and your family and friends. In time, your interests will no doubt expand beyond what is directly in front of you. This book contains many constructive actions to choose from and begin with. The author Ghosh, mentioned earlier, suggests the need to "recover our original reverent and catastrophizing selves who knew how to

motivate in relation to earth's unpredictable episodes."[20] We
have entered unpredictable times. Ghosh's encouraging message
means that we modern humans have it in us to activate in relation
to danger, even though we have been normalized by safety and
an expectation of regularity.

The times they are a-changing, and
a healthy and more respectful relationship with nature
is called upon.

No matter where we live, *we are all,* super-wealthy or not, at the
mercy of Mother Nature, whether it be food scarcity, floods,
storms, or drought. Feeling the feelings around all this is crucial.
Interrupting the momentum of busy life is the only way to make
space for these feelings and recognizing our mutual intercom-
nectedness. Such a change of heart empowers us toward finding
and enacting solutions. Moving forward in the face of the climate
crisis lurking in the background of our awareness feels good. This
unshackled attitude of feeling good beats wallowing in despair
any day and restores enthusiasm for a more hopeful future.

Are you ready to change? Perhaps the summer of 2017 and the
fires and drought of 2018 are enough to shake people up to the
sense of our predicament. Then this book could happily be
unnecessary. I hope so. But on the off chance that people go back
to sleep and forget about the huge wake-up calls, these thoughts
will linger on paper and in the ethers for you to revisit. These

---

[20] Ghosh, Amitav. The Great Derangement. Climate Change and the Unthinkable.
University of Chicago Press. 2016.

words can help you step out of overwhelm and impossibility into concrete measures. Together little pieces of actions from us all accumulate into substantive change.

> *No more important moment has arisen*
> *for placing your trust in the power*
> *of our collective imaginations*
> *and "strategies" we call forth.*

> *When enough people put energy and attention to the challenge,*
> *potential and possibility become probability.*

Such abundant resources have never before been available. Technology is changing so quickly, it's hard to imagine what will be within a short time. Taking back some of my power during this momentous juncture helps me. I examine my life, make changes and help others to also lower the impact of carbon emitted. Being part of solutions is worth celebrating. Be courageous enough to align with the many, many other people positively reworking how we do things.

Imagination

A Story

*The truth is, the single biggest uncertainty in climate science
has nothing to do with the physics of the atmosphere,
or the stability of the ice, or anything like that.
The great uncertainty is, and has always been,
how much carbon pollution humans are going to choose
to pump into the air.*
—Justin Gillis[21]

How much we choose indeed. Ian Dunlop and David Spratt are authors who write, "Climate change is an existential risk that could abruptly end human civilization because of a catastrophic 'failure of imagination' by global leaders to understand and act on

---

[21] Justin Gillis, "The Real Unknown of Climate Change: Our Behavior," *The New York Times*, September 18, 2017.

the science and evidence before them."[22] So far, we are largely failing in our imaginative realms.

We don't have to be part of such failure. To step out of that mindset, we need to activate what psychiatrist and historian Robert Lifton calls, "the evolutionary achievement (of) our human mind (to) imagine beyond the immediate."[23] Immediate challenges though, combine dual predicaments—the scale of global climate change, and a human inability to imagine a state of not being. You're not alone if you can't envisage the end of existence. Self-preservation designed us to keep on keeping on— to continue re-imagining ourselves by holding onto a familiar sense of surviving each new situation which arises. The immense nature of the changing climate, however, does not lend that familiar sense of surviving, nor do we see feasible and complete solutions on the horizon. Even so, answers are not far away, nor are they impossible to discover. We simply must find the news reports beyond the uninspiring news in the mainstream. We need to be inspired so that we can imagine another future.

The power of imagination. Here's a little game for you who are unable to get beyond the enormity of climate change. Imagine yourself as a vigorous, creative and resourceful five-year-old whose world is before you and where anything is possible. Play act in your mind a scenario of what you will do as conditions around you are changing. Remember, you are five years old and you are creative. Anything is possible for you. But first you look around and size up things before you get started. Then you begin simply with modest

---

[22] Ian Dunlop and David Spratt, "Disaster Alley: Climate Change, Conflict and Risk, June 2017.
[23] Bill Moyers, "Despite Trump's Posturing, Americans Are Embracing Climate Change Realities," September 21, 2017.

goals—imagining using less of what you ordinarily consume and reusing what you have so it lasts longer. Think of all the inventive ways you can reuse these things. Picture a game of finding how to make your world cleaner and safer. See yourself discovering strategies to help you both live your life and put less carbon into the air. You are five, after all, and don't really know about carbon, but pretend that you do. You are excited to tell your friends about this new game of using your old stuff differently. You tell your parents. Notice what you feel as you play this game.

Present day you understands this scenario as a game which can be played right now. No need to wait. Look at what your friends have already accomplished. Talk to them and listen to their satisfaction about their new choices. See yourself figuring out solutions that fit you and your family. Imagine how one tiny step will propel your curious self to make more small changes, and think of how these will encourage you to solve even greater challenges. Imagine feeling good about all this.

Next, in your mind's eye envision a faraway land in the not too distant future, a land where people's lifestyles put themselves and others at risk. Visualize them truly feeling the horror of knowing their past actions pushed danger onto their children and grandchildren. Then listen in your mind's ear as these people say, "We can't allow this. We must change how we live now. Let's get started." Do you hear in your mind's ear their enthusiasm at coming together to build new solutions for living and for respecting each other? Imagine your feelings as you eavesdrop.

Picture this scenario coming true for you right now.

CHAPTER 3
A Broad Perspective

I am not "worried about the rising sea
because I believe that in twenty or thirty years,
someone is going to find a solution for this."
—Jorge Perez
Miami's biggest real estate developer in 2017

Let's take a broad view of the remarkably regenerative earth we call home. The earth has such a profound system of continual restoration, where nothing is wasted and everything has a reason for being. Think of the intricate relationships between muscles and ligaments and bones and organs in your body. Complex and all linked with the principle of a healthy functioning body. The planet enjoys the same interrelationship, but the human quest to make living easier and better has interfered with its plan of mutual support and alignment. We waste, we throw out, we make stuff which never goes away, and now more and more people want what has been shown to them as a supposedly better life. When multitudinous people lust after the goods of the developed world, a thorny problem arises, for they enhance their lifestyles by following similar routes of development. The only true home for all of us is Earth. There is only one earth to support us, and this one and only Earth has been damaged. Restoring it takes a while; it does not happen overnight, nor does it heal in weeks or months. Often tens of years (try hundreds) are needed.

A little history of human damage to various places, along with the repair when men and women worked together to resolve those damages, illustrates what I'm getting at. The Hudson River remains polluted, but now less so, with the harmful PCBs (polychlorinated biphenyls) released into the river between 1947 and 1977. Activists stood up and drew attention to the ongoing contamination and risk to human health and the environment. The Environmental Protection Agency (EPA) eventually designated the river as a Superfund site needing remediation. With decades of attention on the Hudson River, the ongoing pollution has ceased, and the water quality has improved greatly. This remediation is one positive turnaround.

The Love Canal in Niagara Falls, New York, presented another instance of changed points of view. Love Canal became a national metaphor for corporate disregard for people in general and for future generations. This tragedy was brought to light in 1976 by investigations into the Hooker Chemical Company which in the 1940's knowingly released tons of various toxic chemicals. Hooker failed to tell residents, whose families were sickened severely enough to abandon their homes. Families moved out, but of course no one wanted to buy these houses, so owners lost everything. After intense activism and consequent litigation, the whole community became a Superfund site, requiring twenty-one years to remediate. The well-known tragedy of Love Canal became a telltale for what happens when inestimable amounts of hazardous industrial products leak from where they should be confined at the work site. Disposing of them properly so they do not harm people in their homes and schools costs money; thus, the toxins were allowed to escape. We can only hope that in the remediation and renaming of Love Canal to Black Creek Village, these same, but so-called less polluted areas are safe and healthy for their new residents. New homes have been built there even while the veracity of this statement is questionable.[24]

Memory is short, yet some of us remember when rivers in the U.S. lit up with fire. The Cuyahoga River in Pittsburg, Pennsylvania, was one of the most polluted rivers in the country. No fish lived in it. A brown oily slick filled with debris hauntingly caught fire in 1969 and everyone was shocked that this could happen in our country. A flood of water pollution control regulations followed this shameful scene and eventually brought about the Clean Water Act, the Great Lakes Water Quality Agreement, the federal Environmental Protection Agency and the Ohio Environmental Protection Agency. These agreements and agencies are the part of the good news to arise from the debacle. Water quality in the river since then has improved and the fish have returned.

Many of us knew long ago about the contributions oil companies were making to climate change. Executives in these companies also knew. What is now common and observable knowledge was

---

[24] "Love Canal Still Oozing Poison 35 Years Later," *New York Post*, November 2, 2013.

proven long ago in the 1970's and 1980's. An eight-month study of Exxon's internal company files revealed ambitious research done about the newly designated 'global warming.' Neela Banerjee, Lisa Song, and David Hasemyer, who investigated the *Inside Climate News* study,[25] also uncovered a consequent misinformation campaign to which Exxon in fact admits. Shannon Hall of *Scientific American Magazine*[26] states about the cover up, "This company employed top scientists to look into the issue of global warming" ... and then "launched its own ambitious research program to empirically sample carbon dioxide and build rigorous climate models. Exxon spent more than $1 million on a tanker project to study how much carbon dioxide was being absorbed by the oceans. This was one of the biggest scientific questions of the time, meaning that Exxon was truly conducting unprecedented research."

However, Exxon and other oil and gas companies subsequently buried the research

because they understood their products would not stay profitable once the research and the risks to the world emerged. The companies promoted diffuse climate misinformation. The argument is familiar. Climate change is not real and environmentalists are un-American when they dispute the 'research' of oil and gas companies. Discrediting information from oil and gas companies about opposing points of view became fodder for confusing the public.

---

[25] Neela Banerjee, Lisa Song, and David Hasemyer, "Exxon, The Road Not Taken," *Inside Climate News*, August 16, 2015.
[26] Shannon Hall, "Exxon Knew About Climate Change Almost 40 Years Ago," *Scientific American*, October 26, 2015.

Muddling the arguments wasted countless years to where now repair and restoration is infinitely more costly, and the results of climate change now harm countless people all over the world. Forty years ago, scientists warned us to take action. They said time was short. Thirty years ago, they warned again, with the caveat that time for significant action was diminishing. And twenty, and ten and now with much less time for repair, they issue similar warnings. Actions so long ago could have turned around climate change harm in less costly ways. Now the expense and the amount of repair needed has grown much greater.

Eventually, each of these old catastrophes garnered attention and then remedial action, except for the fossil fuel misinformation campaigns which continue to this day. Attention and repair are good outcomes to the calamities of old. However, at this time, we no longer have twenty or thirty years to mess around arguing rather than taking stock and acting.

Still, optimists such as Jane Goodall exist to fortify our resolve. In a recent talk at the University of Rhode Island she said, "I still have hope...in the young people who know the problems and are empowered to take action." This famed British primatologist, messenger of peace, and perhaps the world's foremost expert on chimpanzees also has hope because of "the endless possibilities and the potential of human intelligence." Goodall continued,

> "Think, of the amazing technologies emerging which can enable us to live in greater harmony with the planet. Think of the ways people are

working to live their lives in more environ-
mentally friendly ways, as they consider the
consequences of little choices made each day—
what to buy, what to eat, what to wear, how it
was made, where does it come from, did it harm
the environment, did it involve cruelty or suffering to animals and people? These are the kinds
of little choices we make each day."

Plenty of evidence abounds for the human contributions to
atmospheric pollution, a well-recognized term for harmful
contaminants added to where they don't belong, in this case, to
the air. This evidence moves us far beyond historical perspectives
of what we have seen; rivers on fire are one thing, ruined homes
and neighborhoods another, but we live in an atmosphere which
surrounds us and whose air we inhale. We can't get away and we
need air for life. Seems like a trap.

Soot doesn't belong in our air, yet you see and smell it when
following a large truck spewing out noxious black fumes which you
don't even want to breathe. This soot is carbon produced by the
incomplete burning of fuel—carbon passing directly into an
atmosphere science says is already filled with too much carbon.
(We'll get to more on this in Chapter 4, The Basics.)

Black sooty carbon is what we briefly see and gag over; unseen
contaminants continuously infiltrate the air we all breathe. You
need to breathe, right? Me too. Black smoke once bellowing out of
smoke stacks everywhere made people ill; then electrostatic
precipitators were installed to filter out pollutants. Industrial

England sickened many residents with noxious fumes mixed into thick fogs. The 'Great Smog' of 1952 killed four thousand people, and thousands of others ended up with respiratory illnesses. In each case people paid attention and resolved those dilemmas. This worst air pollution event in the United Kingdom led to another good outcome with the UK Clean Air Act of 1956. The issue was that many people's lives were damaged before the act required change. Acting afterwards and sometimes too late is a problem.

These old-time disasters are important to read about because many of us stubborn beings seem to need to be hit over the head before we get the dimensions of the problem and eventually take action. PCBs in the Hudson became a life-altering event for the folk singer Pete Seeger, who spent much of his life singing and campaigning to clean up the Hudson River.

> I am grateful to Seeger, love his heartfelt music, and
> yet we don't have a lifetime in which to get going.
> *We may have twenty years to bring our act together*
> before the challenges meeting us become especially difficult
> to resolve without great effort and radically changed lifestyles.

Twenty years? Think, how short is this time frame. What were you doing twenty years ago? It wasn't very long ago, was it? So much has happened since then (how did we ever get along without iPhones?), but still it's not a long span of time in the greater understanding of the ages. Of course, 20 years is a very long time ago if you were not even born then. All joking aside, this amount of time to remedy something as substantial as a risk to human life does not make not a pretty picture.

All that said about our time frame, unknown and massive opportunities lie waiting within this brief window of great crisis. Opportunities wait upon our response. Long ago, results arose when people took action. Stinking rivers cleared up, fish swam the rivers again, horribly noxious air disappeared, and fewer children developed asthma (this is changing again). People accomplished these great amendments back then and we, the people, can do it again. Simply, now the stakes are higher and there is little leeway.

May the summer of 2017 be the big hit
which propels us into action.

Harmful effects of new and old human influences continue, of course. Methane, a potent greenhouse gas, leaks out in great quantities from far-flung and hard-to-monitor oil wells and gas pipelines in production.[27] Industry has cited a 1% leakage from their sites, seemingly well below the 3% deemed by experts as allowable. However, Gaby Patron, a scientist from the National Oceanic and Atmospheric Agency (NOAA) in Boulder, Colorado, was surprised one day to find more powerful emissions nearby. Her astonishment led her to set out on a two-year study to sample the Denver basin.[28] She found an average of 4% emissions leakage at well sites. Mark Bittman, an investigator for the Public Broadcasting Studios (PBS) production "Years of Living Danger-ously," spent a year expanding Patron's search by crossing the country to study on-site emissions from highly touted clean

---

[27] Mark Pittman, "Chasing Methane, Years of Living Dangerously," Public Broadcasting Service, January 28, 2017.
[28] Cooperative Institute for Research in Environmental Sciences (CIRES): Air Quality Study in Utah, February 18, 2012.

natural gas production. He found these sites to be anything but clean, as rates of 11% in Utah and 17% in Los Angeles jumped out at him.[29] These figures are important because not only do the well heads release gases, but thousands of miles of potentially leaking pipelines cross the country and interlace every city. These leaks add up. Especially as displaced residents of Lawrence, Andover and North Andover, Massachusetts recently discovered when pipelines exploded into flames which engulfed their homes.

These wellhead leaks are only one instance of this strong greenhouse gas entering our atmosphere. Major methane emissions are spewing out of once solidly frozen permafrost tundras of the far north. A warming planet is thawing carbon-dense tundra soils composed of long-dead vegetation and peat. These were once bound into the ice-bound permafrost— thought to be safely entombed, but no. Now these millions of acres of permafrost are melting and quickly releasing vast quantities of methane and carbon dioxide into the air.

We don't know the consequences of this much methane set free, because this gas is seventy-two times more potent in its heat-trapping abilities over a twenty-year period than the carbon dioxide which is universally considered the major greenhouse gas problem.[30] Seventy-two times more potent? Wow. If there is any good news in the report, it is that methane is shorter-lived and remains in the atmosphere for a mere *twelve years,* instead of the hundreds if not thousands of years in which carbon dioxide

---

[29] Op. cit.
[30] Patti Nyman, *Methane vs. Carbon Dioxide: A Greenhouse Gas Showdown.* www.onegreenplanet.org September 30, 2014.

remains. The issue with these timeframes is the very brief window in which to turn our planetary ship around.

Our atmosphere. Millions of acres of methane, layered on top of carbon dioxide, pose a tough equation to figure out. Which to focus on first? Can we afford any of this gaseous mess infiltrating the air we breathe? Can we wait for a response to these questions? My answer is no! Only so much room is available in the mix of a delicately balanced atmosphere composed of 21% oxygen, 78% nitrogen, .93% argon, .04% carbon dioxide, and small amounts of other gases. Odd as it seems because we take for granted the air we breathe, jumbling up these percentages of gases endangers the whole incredibly fine-tuned system of support for life on Earth. Too much of one ingredient crowds the others in the atmosphere and makes for a combination which may not support life. Take a look at the other planets already explored in our search for habitable ones. None has yet been found.

We'd better protect this band of breathable air, surrounding and shielding the earth and her inhabitants from the sun's excessive ultraviolet rays. The atmosphere also retains heat, warms the earth, moderates daytime and nighttime temperatures, and contains varied amounts of water noticed as fog, clouds, rain, snow, or lack thereof. The earth is an incredible living body and we truly have no idea how our interference will play out.

When too much carbon fills the atmosphere, oceans step in to absorb it. Rain pulls carbon out of the air and drops it onto farmlands and onto us as acid rain. Rains fall into rivers which flow the carbon into already dangerously acidic ocean waters which are in turn damaging sea life. Whole ecosystems around dying coral reefs are affected by the acidic oceans. Everything is connected and everything matters.

Quite simply, too many of us drive too many cars and too many factories produce overly numerous plastic products like cell phones and baby toys and plastic plates and on and on. We demand innumerably more of everything, and do not conserve enough resources. To top it off, we don't take enough care with disposing of our stuff. Our desires and the production of more stuff means more carbon dioxide released into the air. We are connected to the dysfunction of our creations.

***

Phew, time to take a break from so much bad news.

Simply breathe in gently and deeply
while you look out at the beauty around you—
the birds, trees, sky, your loved ones.
Look at the grasses glowing and softly backlit
by late day's slanted sunlight.
Take time between bouts of somber words,
to feel your body relax—to notice as goodness returns in you.

This powerful practice becomes more and more essential as the challenges in life multiply. Restoring and re-invigorating yourself is not an airy fairy tale. It is the way to take care of yourself and to handle the bad news by laying a foundation of feeling good inside yourself. Breathe in the good, rest in it, and then dip into the pages again. The poet, Mary Oliver, who really knows about resting in the good, tells you more.

I do not know what gorgeous thing
the bluebird keeps saying,
his voice easing out of his throat,
beak, body into the pink air
of the early morning.
I like it whatever it is.
Sometimes it seems the only thing in the world
that is without dark thoughts.
Sometimes it seems the only thing in the world that is without
questions that can't and probably never will be answered,
The only thing that is entirely content
with the pink, then clear white morning and,
gratefully, says so.[31]

Rest and breathe.......

---

[31] Mary Oliver, *Blue Horses*, (New York: Penguin, 2016)

The belief we can't have a significant effect is one of the barriers to moving forward usefully. This view is why it's time now to look at what is working and at the numbers of people making a difference in their unique ways. There is so much of this to share, but unfortunately you have to look hard for the good news because it doesn't sell as well as does the sensational bad news. Even so, good news is happening.

There's a man in rural India who invented a light powered by the friction of a weight on the end of a rope. The resistance of a mass falling generates enough electricity to power a light bulb at the cord's extremity. This simple, inexpensive invention helps people who cannot afford electricity. Their children's activities don't have to end with the fall of night. Their sons and daughters can study, better themselves and perhaps have healthy lives. All this from one man solving a pressing need for light at night.

The solar world is expanding remarkably. Between 2005 and 2015 the price of solar panels fell over 60% from $8.82 to $3.36 per watt. For sure it's lower still in 2018. The visionary entrepreneur Elon Musk rolled out solar roofing that looks like a traditional roof. More people will install solar roofing because it meshes in with the average house appearance. The side effect of solar panels on a roof consist of money returned to the homeowner, and carbon-free electricity, which gains even more so as power companies enlist more renewable resources.

Solar is now comparable with oil-powered electricity. Home solar system expenses, with tax credits, run between $8 and $14,000 and then your electricity is free *forever*. Solar companies are offering leasing programs with very little up-front costs. This component makes installing solar panels a no-brainer. We all benefit. Solarcity is one example, with a good loan program which I used. They are but one installer, but what I liked about them was seeing their employees feeling enthusiastic about working at a company where they are making a genuine contribution to a better world. Everyone wins when people choose to be proactive where they work, with their purchases, and with their actions.

Solar companies work hard to attract people to lead the way in adopting solar at this early stage of development. The success of these early adopter models shows the feasibility for many homeowners and carbon-free industries to capture the sun on their roofs so they lower fossil fuel use.

The storage of renewably sourced electricity is a major advancement. Intermittent solar and wind production has hindered their wider use because of the need for consistent electricity. But now Elon Musk has come up with a solution. The powerful Tesla PowerWall Charger[32] stores electricity for seven days so that it is available on cloudy days, at night and during storms when the traditional power supply is severed. The technology is here. Now each person has an opportunity to protect the very thin belt of air needed by all creatures on earth. Progress happens when we say 'yes' to what is available. The extra added benefit is, it feels good to be part of the solution.

Here's another piece of good news. California is the poster child for addressing climate change. Perhaps the heady atmosphere of

---

[32] Tesla PowerWall Charger www.tesla.com.

many people there working to improve climate situations inspired one man in Altadena. He wanted residents to adopt Community Choice Aggregation (CCA) as a strategy to gain local control of their power sources.[33] He persevered with town authorities to where residents linked together their solar production to gain renewably sourced and lower cost energy for their community. One single man persisted with his quest and made a difference to his town and to the world. One person at a time, groups of thoughtful townspeople, companies, inventors and foresighted investors are changing the world. This is, indeed, good news.

Next let's look at another imaginary scenario of people thinking together about just this.

---

[33] Peter Kalmus, "Community Choice Energy in L.A. Began with a Single Citizen," *YES! Magazine*, Fall 2017.

Conjure This
A Story

On a late September morning, 16-year-old Celine angrily sloshed through ankle-deep water in the streets of her small town in coastal Florida. "Damn, I forgot to look at the tide chart and didn't bring my boots. Now I have to sit in school all day with this yucky water on me." Mid-muttering, she shrieked as a fish bumped her leg.

"Sheesh, this is just so not right. How come no one is talking about why the streets flood each day? How can they ignore this? It's inconvenient, probably not healthy and for sure, bad for business. It's bad for me."

Celine thought a moment as she splashed along, and continued to herself, "I can't wait for people in charge to motivate themselves. I have to do something. But what can I do? Where do I begin?"

That very afternoon Celine jumped into action to call her friends and talk about the flooding and other changes she had been noticing. Her friends were also upset about it, so she suggested,

"Let's get together tomorrow at Sunrise Beach to talk—around 11? Okay?"

Saturday arrived warm, with a beautifully clear sky, perfect for the beach. Celine gathered her beach bag and happily set off to meet up with Mary and Crystal along the way. How refreshing the briny, pungent salt air felt in her nostrils as they neared the beach. Crashing waves washed away anything but peacefulness in Celine's mind. Warm sand invited her toes.

Ahhhh, all is well, Celine thought to herself. Patreece and Sammie also joined them in the search for a good spot free of stones and near the waves. They laid out blankets and laughingly raced for the water, splashing each other as they ran in. They swam around, rode the waves and hailed to other friends. Finally, tired and chilly, they got out of the water and flopped back on their towels to dry off. Snacks and naps were in order as they relaxed in the sun and melted into the sand.

After resting Celine told her story to begin the conversation she wanted to have. She told about her shock at the fish bumping into her legs. She put into words her anger at the bother of having to remember to check tide charts for when to steer clear of the water-filled streets most anywhere these days. "It is becoming impossible to avoid," she moaned. "So what I need to keep in mind is to bring those stupid boots."

Mary chimed in, "Yeah, I don't like having to lug my boots around all day. They're heavy and clunky. They look dorky and there's not much room in my locker."

"So what's up with all this water? It's supposed to be out there."
Patreece pointed out to the ocean. "Why do you suppose this is
happening? Water in the streets is not the way it used to be. The
tide is just coming in every day and no one talks about it. People
accept it as normal; in fact, it is so normal someone put a giant
ruler on the street to measure the depths of the freakin' water.
Like that's going to help. These high tides are messing up my life.
And my dad complains about salty water ruining his car and
corroding his lawn mower. My brother says his bike is rusty now.
Everybody's having to remember to get their stuff out of the way.
Stuff that used to be safe on lawns or side streets."

Crystal agreed. "Yeah, I don't like it either, but what are we going
to do? The tide comes in and what can we do about that. It's
nature."

Celine countered, "This is not simply nature—and we can do
something about it."

"What, are you crazy? Come on," whined Mary.

"No," Celine answered, "I've been reading about changes
everybody can make. Small things that unfortunately won't help
right away with the tides in the street, but little by little, lots of
people can join in and change the reasons for what is happening.
I've been reading where some people say it is global warming that
causes more water in the air and in the streets. More water in the
air brings on heavier rains and bigger storms. Some call global
warming 'climate change' and say the way we live is causing it.

Just look at that last hurricane. Phew. We don't need those. My parents say they were never in one that bad. Scary."

"Yeah," said Mary, "but what can we do? What does that mean anyway about 'the way we live'? I feel so discouraged about the size of the problem. Especially when no one is paying attention. Sheesh, we can't even mention climate change here in this state. Telling us what we can or can't say really doesn't seem right. Isn't this the home of the free? Besides, it seems just plain stupid when we see big changes happening all around us."

Every girl agreed. "Yes, it's too big, there is nothing we can do. If the grownups are not paying attention, what can we possibly do?"

"But wait," Patreece snapped back, "here's a different thought. Are we also the 'no ones' who aren't aware and the 'no ones' who do nothing?" She mused a few moments. "Hmmmm, I don't want to be a 'do nothing about it' kind of person. And we needn't be. There are things we can do, and we can learn about what's out there for us to know about climate change. We can learn what's realistic for us to do. When we learn, we can act."

Celine agreed. "We can't afford to give up." She stopped and thought before going on. "From what I'm reading, everything is at stake. I mean everything, and no one has even really begun to speak to the enormity of what seems to be coming. These sunny day flood waters will get even deeper. Just imagine what can happen if we get a big storm, or even a small one at the high tide, for that matter."

Sammie considered the conversation. "It's too easy to be discouraged," she added. "We should experience the gloomy feelings—they matter because they're real and they are your very own. But the challenge after feeling them is to keep our hopelessness under control enough so it doesn't overwhelm us. Then we can be part of the solution. This whole mess is huge and we don't know the answers. However, I know I feel better when I do something, rather than sit around feeling bad and hopeless about it."

"That's right," Crystal chimed in. "I read somewhere, it's possible to bounce back and forth between hopelessness and feeling stronger and more confident.[34] It's all in the way we use our positive actions. I read that you can have both feelings until eventually you come to a more stable place of being part of something worthwhile; in this case, progressing steadily toward significant change. I also hear that dancing between feelings like this and then joining with others shifts us out of a stuck place. I like the sounds of these good tactics."

Celine agreed. "I like that too, Crystal. Great thoughts. So this is why I invited you all to talk…. Well, of course it was also to go to the beach." She smiled. "But even more to talk about what no one else is mentioning. Gotta get it out in the open. This is so important it's no longer okay to hide and be silent. Our feelings matter. If we are upset, angry and discouraged, so are others."

---

[34] Patricia Hinkley, *Claiming Space/Finding Stillness that Inspires Action.* (My Five Streams, 2014)

Crystal continued to reflect. "I think we and the folks we encounter will feel better when we talk through our feelings about the changes we all are experiencing. Everyone must be noticing the many changes that are hurting people, their families and friends all over the country. Sharing our feelings leads each of us to a glimmer that there is something we can do. I'm getting the sense as I talk, that together we can help each other."

After hearing this, Celine challenged them. "Are you game?"

Mary said, "Yes, there is a lot to let people know about. I read where residents are putting solar panels on their roofs. Some of them are forming groups to talk about the changing times. Some are beginning to join their solar energy as a community production because their collected energy continues to work even when the power company goes down in a storm. And," she added, "they're powered by the sun and don't add more carbon pollution to the air. It's all good."

Patreece suggested, "It's very good. In fact, we could even talk to our parents about the forbidden term 'climate change' and talk together about solutions that are already out there. Maybe using those words is like saying 'shit mom' when we were five and wanted to shock our parents. But seriously, we can talk to other friends and call people we know in other states. We could start a movement of people talking, thinking of ideas, and standing up for them and for each other. .... and it will begin with us kids. Gosh, I feel better just talking like this."

Celine said, "You know I have a friend in Rhode Island who told me about a group she's part of. They're creating a handbook of do-able strategies for people to take on. She told me there is so much we can accomplish. We don't have to wait for governments to act and to tell us what to do. We can make a difference right now."

"Wow, that's awesome," said Mary, "so we don't have to invent it all ourselves?"

"No," Celine answered, "but since you mention it, invention especially matters these days. So many helpful new ideas are quickly coming to life. We need to study up and learn about them. Then we'll have more to tell our friends and parents and who knows who else. There's a whole lot of enthusiasm in the creative world. Imagine if we challenged our nerdy friends to think bigger than their endless video games and the next shiny gadgets. I guess we'd have to say it better than that, but you know what I mean. They are really smart and when they study and understand the scale of what we are talking about, I betcha they will come up with ways to make big changes. If they try…. scratch that… when they try."

"So what's our next step?" Patreece asked.

CHAPTER 4
The Basics

We cannot solve a problem that we will not face.
With awareness, everything is possible.
Once we stop denying the hard truths
of our environmental collapse,
we can embark on a journey of transformation
that begins with the initial trauma—the 'oh shit' moment—
and can end with transcendence.
In fact, despair is often a crucible for growth.
When our problems seem too big for us to tackle,
there's really only one solution, which is:
We must grow bigger.
—Mary Pipher[35]

I promised to intersperse the good with the bad and the ugly—so here goes a heavy dollop of the ugly. Can you imagine feeling the helplessness, the hopelessness of those who have been victimized

---

[35] Mary Pipher, *The Green Boat: Reviving Ourselves in Our Capsized Culture.* (New York: Riverhead/Penguin, 2013)

by Hurricanes Harvey, Irma, or Maria or by the fires in Montana, California's wine country, San Diego, metropolitan Los Angeles, or by the repeatedly flooded-out towns along the big midwestern rivers?

Failing to acknowledge what has become clearly obvious only intensifies the anguish of those victims. For them it may feel like a dystopian world indeed when the causes of their upside-down reality are denied. I mention these tragedies because we resonate more with our common situation in the United States than we do with the millions of people flooded out in Bangladesh and the climate change afflicted places in Southeast Asia. Of course, these far away people matter a great deal, and yet, seeing people who live in states near you or where you know someone brings it home more personally... perhaps...we hope...

The issue is, these big storms with a chance of striking once in 100 or 500 years are no longer rare. Something is driving their intensity and frequency. The corresponding component to the issue is: we human beings are in the way of change. To begin with, let's take a look at the basics of climate change.

You know how each day the sun warms our earth, which in turn reflects most of its heat back into space? Some of this heat trying to get off the planet is blocked by what are known as greenhouse gases - carbon dioxide and methane in the air. This blockage leads to more heat remaining on the earth. The earth heats up. Crops wilt. Soils dry up. People wither.

As you may or may not know, fossil fuels, coal, oil, and natural gas produce these greenhouse gases. The more oil and the more gas humans use creates a well-known progression of cause and effect amongst the climate change ingredients. Corporations produce oil and gas; people use oil and gas; carbon dioxide escapes into the atmosphere.

Increased carbon dioxide elevates the levels of greenhouse gases which hold in the earth's heat. This retained heat is melting ice on the planet more often and sooner. Fewer light surfaces are available from the once vast ice sheets to reflect heat back into space. The dark ground underneath the former ice absorbs more heat—much like dark clothes make you hot in summer. When once iced-in glaciers melt in conjunction with land areas in Antarctica and all over the world, waters from these no-longer-frozen places raise sea levels.

To complicate matters, the trapped heat also warms the ocean floor and it melts parts of once-frozen tundra soils in the far north. A warmer planet means more moisture evaporates into air which then brings stronger rains to some places and more droughts elsewhere. This is an escalating dilemma because, thawed out permafrost in the tundra lands exhales more heat-trapping methane. Even if we all stopped using fossil fuels today, the already released greenhouse gases will continue to hold in heat and warm the earth for many, many years ahead. This is why it matters so much to stop producing more greenhouse gases now.

Carbon dioxide levels entering the atmosphere must decline.
Fifteen to twenty years
is the window of opportunity for changing the trajectory of
climate change.[36]

What we do in this scant time period matters greatly.

The course of climate change leads to unforeseen effects. The
speed of this process of change is a new and unexpectedly sudden
turn of events. We didn't know the tundra would melt as quickly
as is now occurring so fast or release the huge quantities of
methane as quickly. We didn't know ice masses in the far south
and north would melt this quickly. We didn't realize vast areas of
the world would dry up so soon. Who could predict the strength
of the storms today?

Scientists can't yet foretell how other so-called "feedback loops"
and unintended repercussions will affect more inputs. What we
can see is a less predictable future within the unknown
consequences of nearly 400,000 acres of thawed peat beneath
the once ice-covered ground. Those who study climate science
cannot now tell in advance the effects of the cascading outcomes.
Science can only surmise potential backlashes.

Another curiosity arises, for who can truly know what else is
possible when thousands of years-old frozen earth melts the
covering of 1/4 of the land in the northern climes?

---

[36] Paul Hawkins, *Drawdown: The Most Comprehensive Book on Climate Change.* (New
York: Penguin, 2017)

We have some ideas about disease molecules
held frozen within the ice.
We have some ideas about the garbage and pollutants from
300 years of industrialization.
Permafrost soils containing bacteria and viruses once frozen
for thousands of years are melting.

"Permafrost is a very good preserver of microbes and viruses, because it is cold, there is no oxygen, and it is dark," says evolutionary biologist Jean-Michel Claverie[37] at Aix-Marseille University in France. Claverie opened the field of Paleovirology after reviving two viruses from 30,000-year-old Siberian permafrost. "Pathogenic viruses that can infect humans or animals might be preserved in old permafrost layers, including some that have caused global epidemics in the past."

An overly hot earth whose weather is erratic enough that farmers can't reliably grow our food creates another unforeseen effect. *The food supply is at risk.* Check out migrating people across Africa.[38]

For sure there will be good adaptations within the challenges.
Even more certain is the fact that challenges will show up.

Aftermaths of warming are presenting themselves already. As the planet warms, the air around the land warms and then more moisture evaporates into the warmer air. Then storms containing

---

[37] Jean-Michel Claverie, Professor of Medicine, Aix-Marseille University. Information Génomique et Structurale.

[38] "Climate Driven Migration in Africa," European Council on Foreign Relations, December 20, 2017.

abundant water rain down in heavier downpours. Remember the extraordinary rains in Houston in the 2017 Hurricane Harvey? Fifty inches of rain? Imagine the estimated 33 *trillion* gallons of water which fell on the affected areas beneath these sodden clouds. An unexpected consequence of this heavy weight is that land in the city of Houston sank by two centimeters![39] Who can guess what a lowered land mass can lead to? Broken buildings for sure, but what else? As this book goes to press in 2018, rainfall in North Carolina is mounting—two feet and still pouring in places. Some towns are entirely cut off from the rest of the state."

Anyway, more moisture in the air leads to stronger storms in some places and to drought in others. Not only are storms more intense, they are more frequent. And all that rain falling in some places seems to squeeze dry other places. These are not scientific statements; they are simply observations of what is happening as you widen your lens to include places where you don't live. Certainly hotter temperatures increase evaporation, and dry the soils due to increased evaporation, which stirs up the air. This disruption increases severe weather conditions which are often aided by air circulation patterns such as El Niño. More water demands from people and agriculture exacerbate drought conditions. Drier soils and drier vegetation allow forest fires to increase in numbers and to spread rapidly.[40] For sure we are witnessing shifting weather patterns.

Many more climate events are happening beyond those in the United States. Already India has lost 24% of its land to

---

[39] Scott Johnson, "The Weight of Harvey's Floodwater Actually made Houston Sink a Little," *Ars Technica*, September 6, 2017.
[40] Richard Restuccia, "5 Causes of Drought," *JAIN magazine*, August 16, 2016.

desertification. Hot land means hotter air. Hot land does not support healthy agriculture. A mere 2% increase in temperature will decrease India's food supply by 1/4—less food for over one *billion* people. For reference, the population of the U.S. is 320 million. Three times the population of the U.S. will have significantly less food. Rivers in China and Southeast Asia from the Himalayas and Tibet sustain 47% of the world's population; yet because of increased warming, Himalayan glaciers have been decreasing since the 1940's. This source of water for half a billion people is projected to disappear by 2050. These numbers are greater than the population of the U.S. without any water supplies. Staggering. Imagine what will happen if that scenario becomes a reality.

All of this supports the thought that no strategy can work globally unless it works in Asia and unless it is adopted by large numbers of Asians. The numbers of people are simply too great. Nor does it work if large numbers of people in the U.S. do not also act. Massive change is only possible when U.S. residents take it seriously enough to show others they earnestly understand the gravity of the situation. The response of business leaders and states to the Paris Climate Accord is a case in point, for they signaled a more comprehensive response beyond the administration's short-sighted view. All of us must work together

Does this make sense to you?

Now is a good time to take a break and breathe again.
Breathe gently and deeply into your belly
and look out at something you love.
No efforting, simply feeling an active expansion within yourself.
And then,
Rest in the light on the clusters of tiny red berries
or the birds flying overhead
or whatever your eye delights in.
Feel goodness and warmth flow into you.
Relax into this inner treasure of calm.
Breathe like this for a few minutes.

This respite is a resource available to you anytime
when you stop to allow it to unfurl its goodness throughout you.
Breathing in this way will serve you well when you do stop for it.

And now come back. It may take reading all this again and it may take more investigation to fully grasp the basics of what is happening with the earth and its climate. There is an abundance of information available to help you understand more. Please do inform yourself. Paul Hawkins, a well-known American environmentalist and author, wrote a substantial resource, *Drawdown:*

The Most Comprehensive Book on Climate Change.[41] Time is short for turning the climate train around, too short for any more of what the climate scientist and captivating speaker Kevin Anderson calls, "contrived ignorance or willful blindness."[42] We need us all together to get moving.

We don't know the overlapping consequences, but for sure we do know there will be many changes where each of us lives as the planet warms. It is going to get hotter. More heat will cause stronger storms, increased droughts, and fires. Increased heat exacerbates discomfort and leads to disabling health conditions for many people.

Add onto these the unknowns spinning out when each stormy, hot event changes the ecosystem around you into an uncharted future. The earth works well with a delicate and finely honed balance. This planet, on whose health we depend, has the capability to restore herself—over time and in her own way. She will do what needs to be done; however, restoration may not be timely for our comfort levels. Look at Puerto Rico, without electricity for months. It's hot there and many people needed oxygen or dialysis or surgery. They needed ordinary, yet life-sustaining medications to which they no longer had access. Air conditioning, refrigeration, hospitals, businesses all require electricity, yet there was none for many people. Limited amounts of power were reserved for the most essential services which

[41]Hawkins, Paul, Drawdown: The Most Comprehensive Book on Climate Change. Penguin Books. 2017. New York, New York.
[42] Kevin Anderson, Gordon Goodman Memorial Lecture. Stockholm, Sweden. September 26, 2017.

could be reached on the tree-clogged roads. It challenges my mind to imagine going without power for so long.

The reason for presenting this very basic level of climate understanding isn't to panic you, but to let you know the situation is urgent. This discourse is meant to disrupt your "normalcy bias" —a false belief we all have about carrying on as we are with things as they have been. Simply put, humans beings must find a way to create fewer greenhouse gases—now! The definition of urgent is a state or situation requiring immediate action or attention. Urgent means words such as 'the need is pressing, dire, acute, serious, desperate.' It means the earth is crying out to us, calling for our earnest and persistent response—calling for us to change how we do things—how we drive, eat, even choosing where to live. It is *urgent* that we pay attention.

Will you hear the call? These enormous storms are certainly attention-grabbing events. I hope they got yours.

The next chapter shows how conditions are getting the attention of a bunch of skiers.

Imagine
A Story

You are not an isolated actor,
living in a stable country on a stable planet,
whose main purpose in life is to pursue personal success,
familial satisfaction, and constant gratification.
Rather, you are living in a country, and on a planet, in crisis.
Your primary moral responsibility is to fight for your family,
your species and all life on earth.
You didn't ask for it, you didn't cause it,
and you probably don't like it.
But here you are.
—Margaret Klein Salamon[43]

Five healthy and well-to-do skiers are sitting around a Jackson Hole lodge reviewing the day's ski conditions, their final runs down the trails and the night's upcoming party.

---

[43] Margaret Klein Salamon, "The Transformative Power of Climate Truth," *Common Dreams*, April 27, 2015.

The conversation eventually drifts to how the snowpack in so many ski areas is not what it used to be. Charlie expands the conversation. "I wonder how a climate-changed future will affect many of our experiences, including not having enough snow for wherever we want to ski."

"Yeah, it's not looking good these days," Sam says. "Tahoe used to have tremendous snowfalls, and now it is unreliable. Sometimes they get a foot of snow and other times bare patches cover the runs. At least Jackson Hole continues to get good powder."

Charlie adds, "Yeah, agreed. It was awesome today. We are so fortunate we can choose where to go when conditions are not great. I wonder how the less fortunate people will fare in a changing climate. They don't have choices about even where to live." He paused. "I wonder what we can do about this? Maybe we can think together about what we personally can do."

Sam agrees. "Yes, I can give lots of money to help people."

Charlie responds, "Yes, Sam that is great, I will do the same… and yet, I suspect each of us is going to have to do more. I do give money to support worthy causes that are figuring out how to resolve climate change. Beyond this, it is time to go further. We need to rethink our individual ways and how we live. The way I understand it, we all are contributing to this problem."

"What do you mean?" Tom enters in.

"Well," Charlie answers, "look at the many plane trips I take. Maybe I needn't fly so much. I could teleconference more, drive to nearby locations, or better yet, take a train."

"The train?" Phil yipes. "It takes so long."

"Yes, it's a bit longer," Charlie laughs, "though not so much really when you think of the whole saga of getting to airports and waiting around." He continued, "I use my time sitting on the train to nap, read, catch up on work, whatever. I actually enjoy the leisure of it. Don't get much empty time where I can choose what or if I want to do anything.

"What I'm saying is," Charlie continues, "we can begin to consider the effects of what we do. Our everyday actions make a difference to everyone else in the world. So many people are suffering the repercussions of climate change; we need to rethink how unknowingly we add to their hardships. Stuff like people moving away from where they can no longer grow food for their families. And so much more we don't even hear about."

"Yeah, I get that," Andrew adds. "What we do and how we live goes way beyond our whims. This is huge. Our choices in the first world where we live have now become a values issue about how we want our fellow human beings to be able to eke out a living and survive." He goes on, "I care about them."

Sam says, "I see what you mean, Andrew. We are fortunate beyond belief and yet we take it all for granted, as if our experiences are normal for everyone. They are not, and I don't feel good about the huge gulf between our good fortune, especially in relation to other people's climate ordeals."

"Neither do I, come to think of it," says Tom.

Charlie continues, "That's a great beginning, Andrew, to consider the consequences of our actions. We all have a moral compass inside us; it's just that the race for money blinds us to thinking of the big picture that involves us all. And then we forget about the rest of the others losing out. However, because the changing climate is real and will impact each one of us, it's time to adjust how we think." He continues the thought. "This whole thing is scary. I want to be able to ski with my kids in the future and I want to be able to eat fish. And the way we are going, neither looks promising unless we begin to treat the whole dilemma as real. I care about it all, and I want to be part of solving this. Because I've been thinking about this a while, I've come to conclude, I don't need all the stuff I endlessly acquire. In truth, I could get rid of some of it, like extra houses, cars and toys."

"Hold on now," Tom interjects, "what you say, fewer toys? I deserve the fruits of my labors."

Charlie responds, "Come on now, Tom—your labors? Ha ha. I'm not talking about suffering here, mind you. Things have gotten so out of hand I know I can scale back a bit, and I can pay more attention to what I acquire. This is a beginning. All this stuff is not making me happier anyway. They are only more things to take care of. Happiness for me comes from being with my family and friends."

"I see your point, Charlie," Sam answers, "but I'm not there yet. I like my things. I earned them, after all. You bring up good points though, and I will continue to think about what we've talked about."

Phil speaks up. "Maybe I'll take the train for yucks. Can at least give it a try. It sounds as if it could be good." Phil hesitates and goes on. "You know, this is one of the more interesting conversations I've had in a long time. Let's continue to talk." They all agreed to meet and carry on the discussion the next day after the last run down the hills.

CHAPTER 5
Urgency

Neither a wise man nor a brave man
lies down on the tracks of history
to wait for the train of the future
to run over him.
—Dwight D. Eisenhower

You may ask, why is the issue of climate change so pressing? Why does it require immediate, earnest and persistent response? Because the climate is in a state of crisis already much more advanced than what we hear on the nightly news.

The Intergovernmental Panel on Climate Change (IPCC) presented their findings at the Paris Climate Accord in 2015:

Warming of the climate system is ***unequivocal***,
as is now evident from observations
of increases in global average air and ocean temperatures,
widespread melting of snow and ice,
rising global average sea levels, and ocean acidification.

These IPCC assessments were based on 2013-14 research which was reviewed and subsequently minimized by organizations, corporations and people looking to continue benefitting from the sale of fossil fuels. Unfortunately, after this historic accord, mainstream news media outlets primarily reported from the perspective of fossil fuel interests vested in continuing their extractive businesses. The good news is that most nations of the world agreed on the IPCC set of timelines.

The IPCC report raises several issues. First, figures used to compute outcomes were based on at best three-year-old information, when in contrast, alterations in the status of the earth are rapidly moving forward. Author David Titley[44] is a professor of meteorology at Pennsylvania State University and also the founding director of the Penn State Center for Solutions to Weather and Climate Risk. Titley noted a problem hidden beneath the celebrations following the agreement made by almost all countries on earth. He wrote in response to the IPCC,

> "Recently a series of scientific papers have come out
> and stated that we have a 5% chance
> of limiting warming to 2°C, and
> *only one chance in a hundred*
> of keeping man-made global warming to 1.5°C,
> the aspirational goal of the 2015 Paris United Nations
> Framework Convention on Climate Change.
> Additionally, recent research shows that
> we may have already locked in 1.5°C of warming
> even if we magically reduced our carbon footprint
> to zero *today*."

---

[44] David Titley, "The 2 degrees that matter most," The Conversation, Salon.com, August 30, 2017.

A problem indeed. Secondly even though this accord is a remarkable agreement amongst many nations about the severity of climate change, what the IPCC assessed is not mandatory or enforceable. Already we see governments wriggling out of making changes in response to what they agreed upon. The third problem is the IPCC calls for changes far off in the next century. The effect keeps people asleep, continuing to use oil and gas as if nothing is wrong, and keeps most of them unworried about how climate change will effect us all. The report reassured them the time for significant change is far away. The watered down IPCC announcement also gave rise to the belief that, for sure *someone* will do something about it. Numerous credible sources suggest possibly much less time to get our act together. A 10% chance exists for temperatures to rise above 4% celsius within 10-30 years. Elevated temperatures along the way will inexorably stress us all; i.e., fry us and our food supply.

To top off these forewarnings,
Professor Hans Joachim Schellnhuber,
Director of the Potsdam Institute for Climate Impact Research
in Germany
used two words to dramatically explain the difference
between a 2°C and a 4°C world:
"Human civilization."

Right, that's us. The World Bank adds emphasis: "There is no certainty that adaptation to a 4°C world is possible." Between 2 and 4° is time for action. This means *now*. The risk for a less favorable outcome increases as we move along this spectrum. Time for dawdling within this window of opportunity has gone by.

This is, however, a good time to stop for a few minutes
and take a breath again—
to create breathing space once again—
to remember the good in your life.
Breathe deeply into your belly and put a little smile on your face.
Breathe in the qualities of patience and kindness.
Remember that you are reading words on a paper—
and there is still much you can do.
Remember this as you dive back into the next paragraph.

Continuing on with the discussion of what is urgent and why it is urgent and paramount. As one of most recognized climate researchers in the UK, Professor Kevin Anderson is able to clearly communicate climate science to decision-makers, the business sector, civil society, and the media. He suggests that the 2% carbon budget, which economists allow for emissions, is a delusion computed by short-term thinking and the desire for power. This budget is premised on an assumption that unknown and untested technologies will work by 2030 and 2050. Anderson says this is a fantasy upon which we cannot base the continuing existence of the world. Carbon emissions, which continue to spike sharply upward, are already 60% higher than they were in 1990. Left alone, without these currently imagined and untested technologies working, emissions will continue to spike 3 to 5% more while temperatures rise 4 to 6°. It's hard to imagine, but the problem is, we don't have 3-5% wriggle room left in a feasible and livable carbon allotment. Many people will die at these temp-eratures if the theoretical plans based on a nightmarish daydream lead to an unsustainable and unsafe threshold. Emissions are unlikely to magically turn themselves around with these far-off and untested solutions. For Anderson, what matters is that the present allowance for carbon budgets will change the climate for several centuries. *Several centuries of possibly 4-degree-higher temperatures.*

> *The conclusion is: technology alone is not enough,*
> *especially imaginary technology.*
> *Here's a baseline truth: people need to change*
> *what we do and how often we do it.*

The radically short timeframe leads Anderson and others to suggest a Marshall-style transition in supply technologies that will bring us to using zero carbon energy in everything we do by 2035. This *seventeen-year* transition will involve massive programs for low-carbon electrification, which in time will be sourced with renewable energies. The programs also will require a transition to the most efficient end-use technologies and stringent efficiency standards. The scale of this energy revolution necessitates profound shifts in behaviors and practices in terms of what we do, and also in terms of a new economic framework which fits the purpose. Companies will be forced to find ways to profit from the new technologies and efforts. When forced by necessity to change, they will discover ways that reduce their energy requirements and consequently lower their costs of doing business. Anderson surmises that an economic perspective, coupled with technology, will help us accomplish the turnaround and achieve the climate goals in three decades.

The state of our climate resolve, for Anderson, is both a moral imperative and an equity issue. Huge amounts of depth work around climate change lead him to live out his suggestions. For one, he studies his carbon footprint and refuses to travel by plane to conferences. He walks, buses, or trains his talk. Anderson says wealthy nations need to be discussing climate change efforts in relation to their place with the rest of the world. We are so interconnected that one nation never exists solely on its own in the world. One nation affects others. Relying on untested technologies, which may well fail, is an ethical hazard where non-white poor people suffer more due to an asymmetry of emissions. Excessive flying is part of the difficulty. Poor communities are being asked to decrease their access to energy in order to safeguard carbon reserves being used up by wealthy fliers. I agree with Anderson that this does not seem fair.

Remember, there is very little room for the wealthy world to continue seeking comfort while more carbon continues to flow into the atmosphere. This is a challenging concept when things seem normal to many people. What I'm trying to get across is that things decidedly are not normal for many others. These are tough decisions, yet …

We, in the developed world, can't have it both ways
because every ton of carbon emitted by flying
takes away a ton of carbon dioxide which poor communities
need to grow, transform and enhance their welfare.
Their demands for energy represent a near-term need,
while rapidly evolving technologies speed their transition
to more sustainable renewables.

Wasteful uses of energy, on the other hand, take away from a finite carbon allotment needed to preserve life on the planet. Wealthy countries can afford to scale back energy uses by 40% in ten years, partly because people in these regions still will be okay. Poorer nations cannot do this at this stage in their development; however, they needn't follow the long road to electrifying themselves. Anderson goes on to speak about equity for what we have messed up. He says wealthy nations need to make reparations for those who cannot possibly fix what the world has wrought upon them. He maintains that we owe this much because we have limited their options. Equity is especially challenging in the profit-only models of business and government.[45]

Thinking ahead and planning from intergenerational perspectives is truly called for. Imagination and focus will guide us in co-creating an eventual zero-carbon future. Our focus and our vision can help us describe what our lives will look like when we reduce energy use. There can be better outcomes for job security, for health, and for the seemingly endless crime in our world. Describing a just transition to an imaginable future offers much more hope than do the dystopian Mad Max novels. If we can imagine it, we will find the ways to accomplish what now seem like miracles. Transforming ourselves will indeed be a miracle worth celebrating. There is plenty we can do and the time is now.

Where are we at this point? In 2017, 50% of global emissions arose from 10% of the world's population. Pretty big imbalance there. Oddly enough, this is good news, for it points a direction forward.

---

[45] Kevin Anderson, Professor of Energy and Climate Change, University of Manchester. Deputy Director, Tyndall Centre for Climate Change Research.

If 10% of global emitters decreased their discharges, we would all benefit. The first order task, then, is to reach out to the 10%. The bad news, as if we needed more, is 7,500,000,000 people want to live like the images they see on television. Seven and a half billion people living as do those in developing countries puts more carbon into the atmosphere than the planet can bear. These billions of people need examples of better ways to get to where they want to be without the precedents provided by the Western world.

The equity issue reframes the whole climate change argument,
for seven and a half billion people in the world
have little opportunity to change their emissions.

The immediate task becomes one of identifying the 10% of the world's population who use excessive oil and gas, so a message can be tailored to them. I suspect we can guess the 10%. I'm not talking about the commonly maligned 1% of the world's wealthiest people. I am talking about you and me and many others in the Western developed world. The task then is simply to help us all see our common dilemma. *No one escapes this mess.*

Once the 10% is identified, vocal visionaries are needed to speak out for changing a system so out of balance. For example, it is time for academics and all of us to hold politicians accountable to the pressing realities. We ourselves must be answerable as well. This is where vocal visionaries can shine. They will help excessive travelers understand the grave consequences of their actions. Many well-meaning people fly too often: climate scientists, academics, policy makers, business people, frequent fliers, vaca-tioners, and audiences. Universities and locations for symposia must rethink their demands. We in the developed world have the great privilege of being able to alter our habits, and it is imperative that we do so. Climate change becomes a huge opportunity for good, an opportunity to create change, to set an admirable model.

It is fascinating to live at this place in time with both a pressing need to change and with exponential changes in technology ushering in expansive potential to turn around what is needed.

HOWEVER,
technology alone will not save us.
Big changes depend on us all,
on each one of us
to get busy and get in the game.

Am I being redundant? Good. Listen. Heads up so you can get going on making changes.

The next chapter shows another group of people tackling the climate issues.

Communication is key.
"100% Renewable" is the new watchword.
It sums up what we need to do:
move off coal, oil, and gas and on to sun and wind.
And it makes it clear it's urgent: we have to go all the way
and we have to do it fast.
No more half measures.
—Bill McKibben

In Your Mind's Eye
A Story

A group of thirty-some-year-old friends are checking their Twitter feeds while they talk about what is happening around them. Nick begins, "My friend's family was flooded out in a freakish storm that rained long enough for rivers to overflow their banks and enter homes along the way."

Sally adds, "My friend in Phoenix can no longer spend much time outside in the summer because of 120-degree days."

Ashley agrees. "Weirdness is happening all around us. My friends are getting asthma from the dust."

Nick says, "I read that someplace in Southeast Asia, maybe Bangladesh is mostly all under water. Crazy, right?"

Each one of these young adults concurs that something eerie and uncomfortable is going on, and it's happening in too many places.

"Yeah, look at this." Chris points to his Twitter feed. "This monster storm just hit Russia and thousands are without power. You don't hear about that on the news."

Megan says, "It seems like something is going wrong nearly every day. It's hard to take it all in."

"Yeah, it makes me feel kind of hopeless about the future," agrees Tyler.

"Well I'm angry about this," Ashley retorts, "angry so much is happening and so little is being done."

Nick asks, "Well, what would you like to be done?"

Ashley says, "I don't know, just someone, somewhere to take leadership and get started. We need someone to get us started. We can't just sit here and drown."

"Well," Nick counters, "who is that someone? Our leaders are doofuses. Who do you think should get us started?"

Sally comes back at them. "I don't think our leaders are capable of much. We have to do this ourselves. We can't rely on them."

"Whaaat," asks Megan. "Hold on, we don't know what to do or even where to begin. There have to be some people who know. And I feel so bad about things happening to the poor folks who get drowned out or have pollution in their backyards. It's just not fair."

"I feel terrible about that too, Megan," Sally answers, "And you bring up good thoughts. We can start off with the question of what can we do? And we can ask—who knows something about what will help? There are people who have been studying this. I bet if we put our minds to it, we can find them. We are very skilled in the ways we communicate." Laughter echoes around the room. "That has to count for something."

"Okay," says Megan, "so let's fish around our concerns on Facebook and Twitter and see who bites. Who shows up and with what should be interesting. And how motivating it is to think together about something important and what we can do about it. I am so bored with looking at selfies and cats. I feel better just making a beginning plan."

"We have lots of resources, too," Chris observes. "Look at the examples of the older generation of environmental activists, scientists and writers, who have been working to preserve the environment and have followed climate developments for many years. I'm sure some of them know where to begin."

"You know what?" says Nick, "I too feel inspired to think we could make a difference. There are plenty of us millennials searching around for meaningful jobs. We feel unhappy with what we are doing and we want to make a difference, yet we can't even support ourselves well. Seizing the opportunities within this changing climate can make the work we do more worthwhile. So if we get started, we can have an impact on the disastrous course of it all and we can even help our generation of floundering friends."

"This makes me feel good," answers Megan. "I care and know I'm not the only one who does!"

"Now that I think about it," adds Sally, "I wasn't paying much attention to my mom the other day, but maybe she has something worth looking into. She saw a movie about conscious companies aligning with their values. The movie described them as good places to work, too."

"Cool, what's that movie?"

"It's called 'Prosperity,'" Sally answers, "and it's online for free right now. We can have a choice and don't have to work for the old models of companies who are destroying the earth. We can look for those doing good."

"You know," Ashley agrees, "business is such a big part of the problem. We just have to stop supporting the ones who are not paying attention to the harm they are doing."

"Lots to talk about after all," says Nick. "Gotta go to that bummer job now, but let's get together again and talk more," as he waves to his friends.

CHAPTER 6
Mobilizing the Good

As we watch the sun go down, evening after evening,
through the smog across the poisoned waters of our native earth,
we must ask ourselves seriously whether we really wish
some future universal historian
on another planet to say about us:
"With all their genius and with all their skill,
they ran out of foresight and air and food and water and ideas," or,
"They went on playing politics
until their world collapsed around them."

—U Thant
Former United Nations Secretary General

The good news is, there are many organizations getting down to work on climate change. A full court press is called for, and entities such as Job One for Humanity, 350.org, TreeofLife.org, Civic Alliance for a Cooler Rhode Island (CACRI), The Climate Mobilization (TCM), and others are gearing up. The underlying message is twofold: we have to change our ways, and there is little time to adapt easily. Bill McKibben says it well in his title, *Winning Slowly is the Same as Losing.*[46] We must act quickly.

Nonetheless, McKibben is still hopeful. He feels inspired by the thought that those who can bear the expenses will take the necessary steps will do so. He urges those homeowners to meet his challenge if they can afford to purchase insulation, solar panels and appliances. For example, Billy Parish is the CEO of Mosaic, the biggest solar lender in the country. The company promises to "make a household operate on 100% clean energy" and to save money from day one while it does so.

The confidence we gain from seeing others responsibly meeting the challenge of climate change will galvanize us. The starting point is to simply step up and become 100% solar.

Plenty of people are able to do this, especially when companies now offer 'no down payment' loans. McKibben also places great hope on the power of movements to "concentrate the minds of CEOs and presidential candidates," in order to stir the sluggish ones into action.

The groups listed in the first paragraph of this chapter all recognize the timeline and understand there is no 'they' who will fix it. These forward-thinking groups are drawing from significant and unbiased climate change investigation. Candid research points to an exponential rise in carbon releases into the atmosphere. Unfortunately, by its very definition 'exponential'

---

[46] William McKibben, "Winning Slowly is the Same as Losing," *Rolling Stone* magazine, December 1, 2017.

means that for a long while nothing is visible; then, at a certain tipping point, the issue becomes highly visible and too unwieldy to stop its progression. The change is not only big, it becomes unwieldy as feedback loops exacerbate one another in the process of carbon and temperatures rising.

Exponential carbon increases drive runaway global warming with incalculable results too vast to easily interrupt. For certain, living as we have known it becomes a thing of the past. At the very least, we will have entered an exceedingly disruptive period. Pioneering organizations foresee a short window of perhaps 20 years. Some say less time is at hand for activating adequately worthwhile changes in the amounts of carbon entering the atmosphere. This is no joke.

Hence the urgency involved in alerting people.
This is me—alerting YOU.

The TCM organization calls for a World War II scale of mobilization. In the World War II era, everyone understood the pressing need and everyone pitched in. A look back in our history shows how rapidly people can transform when they recognize the emergency. TCM intends to activate people to join together to "protect civilization and the natural world." Their plan is to "reach net zero greenhouse gas emissions nationally in ten years or less, and globally by 2030, to restore a safe climate for humanity, by drawing down excess carbon in the atmosphere." Hmmm, why are they so concerned?

According to TCM, famine, drought, state failures and mass species extinctions which are already under way (the last known male rhinoceros just died) have the potential to profoundly backlash on civilization in ways which bring on climate chaos in our lifetimes. While most Americans know about climate change, few people tell the whole story about the scale and the need for swift action. Meanwhile, months and years go by while carbon silently and relentlessly builds up in the air and the oceans. The ones who fail to tell the complete truth about climate change say they are afraid to frighten people...better to keep it quiet. They may have other motives, but their attitude points to one point of view about human nature.

TCM expects though, when people see "they and their children are profoundly threatened by runaway global warming—they would want to do everything possible to save humanity from this fate." This is why they call for a loud and grand mobilization to get people's attention away from their distractions. The goal, by acting now, is to curb what causes greenhouse gas emissions, limit dependence on fossil fuels, and to lessen the devastating effects from global warming.

We are not lacking in the dynamic forces
needed to create the future.
We live immersed in a sea of energy beyond all comprehension.
—Thomas Berry, The New Story[47]

---

[47] Thomas Berry, priest, leading cultural historian, ecotheologian and author of *The New Story*. (first published in *Teilhard Studies*, no. 1, 1978)

The power of the human spirit is compelling. Substantial outcomes are possible when we collectively mobilize. Look at the recent example of the speed of the "Me Too" movement against sexual harassment and assault, which catalyzed action in a timeframe never imagined possible. If people can come together in this way, mobilizing can happen around climate reordering. Perhaps the greatest result is that joining together empowers us to take on more. When each of us educates ourselves about the speedily changing climate and its effects on the many people across the globe, we learn both about technological expertise and exponential developments to share.

Climate change has become a serious policy issue for almost every country on the planet, except for the U.S. Government, whose leadership has decided to ignore climate change, remove all mention of it in agency documents, and even to reverse progress made thus far. Constructive governmental prioritizing around climate issues would greatly help a mobilization; however, lacking this, we citizens, corporations, state and local governments are being called to step forward. We are summoned to become accountable to one another. This is something we can join with.

Let's move on to some positive news of what forward-looking organizations are up to. There is so much good to discover about people and technology and states and companies stepping up with unique solutions. California's Global Warming Solutions Act of 2006 (AB 32) models how to move forward quickly and to set an absolute statewide limit on greenhouse gas emissions. My hope is that the short-sighted vow from the current administration to rescind this act will be challenged and defeated, for this act confirms the state's commitment to transition to a sustainable, clean energy economy and a healthier future. California had already raised its goal for 2030 to achieve greenhouse gas emissions at 40% below 1990 levels. Legislation in 2015 required the state to increase its renewable energy mix to 50% and to double energy efficiency in existing buildings by 2030. Impressive outcomes are turning up from the first decade of this serious implementation.

Innovative advancements in clean energy and efficiency are moving California well on its way to the renewable energy targets. To boot, the state economy is growing while carbon pollution is declining. California has caused a ripple effect where Washington, New York, Colorado and states in New England are following in its footsteps. The County Council of Montgomery County, Maryland, unanimously passed a first-in-the-nation resolution declaring a climate emergency. The Council also moved its emissions reduction goals from 80% by 2050 to 100% by 2035. These regions show us climate action can move forward admirably, in spite of a lagging national government.

Green, non-fossil fuel energy initiatives produce good American jobs and bolster America's global leadership in clean energy innovations. Just look at the sea of thousands of wind turbines in California's windy San Gorgonio Pass or the turbines along Pennsylvania's Allegheny ridges. Look at the millions of rooftop solar panels everywhere. Look to Elon Musk's Tesla Powerwall home batteries[48] providing backup energy by day or night and when the wind levels are low. Batteries which stabilize energy

---

[48] https://www.tesla.com/powerwall.

received by sun or wind are revolutionary enough to make a huge difference for the renewable industry. Reliable energy day and night makes us more independent of external power sources and of the need for building new 'peak use' power plants which insure continued use of fossil fuels and carbon increases we cannot afford. This is sweeping change indeed.

We have not yet arrived where we have no need for fossil fuels, but we are certainly in a transition phase. We will most likely always need petroleum products for essential supplies like medical tubing. Nonetheless, each clean energy innovation vitalizes both demand and competitiveness for manufacturing and constructing components.

Green energy projects are sustainable and reduce a country's reliance on finite and non-replaceable natural resources. Substituting antiquated power generated by carbon fuels with green technologies is one of the fastest ways to reduce greenhouse gas emissions. Fastest because the technology is already here and the costs have come down dramatically. Hence, the urging for people to step up, use what is at their fingertips, and then talk about it. Spread the word. The technology is at hand. Please use it!!

I write so much about technology because it's here, available, ready to use, and it's glitzy. The tech world would have us believe this is all we need. However, there is more to consider because technology is not the whole answer. What really matters for me is that we allow our hearts to touch the depths of the conundrum. Then feelings based on this greater understanding will lead us on.

Heart is key to it all—to meaning, to action, to connection.
And each of us has one of these whiz bang marvels.
Try it out.

The missing piece in a grand plan of mobilization is that "everyone understand the pressing need" and the emergency.

This list shows what is possible when people engage from a place of heartful resonance and action.

- Canada is waiting in the wings with abundant low-carbon electricity ready to send into the U.S. That big country to the north runs on almost 60% hydropower and has more clean electricity than it can use. Its green power will help states in the Northeast meet their goals for achieving clean energy. Utility companies in Canada propose to build new transmission lines to power New York state and to become "the battery of North America." Canada wants to use their excess electricity as our backup to prevent the construction of peak energy usage power plants. This is, of course, an economic strategy as well as good intentions, plus it is also neighborly and of huge benefit to the world.

- Miami is a city in trouble. It is recognizing the problems and changing to work with the environment rather than against it. South Miami now requires all new homes to have solar panels. Miami taxpayers voted for a "Miami Forever" bond issue to tax themselves to protect the city and neighborhoods from sea level rise.[49]

- South Australia was in dire need of energy storage after a series of massive storms left 1.7 million people in the dark. Elon Musk, CEO of SpaceX and Tesla Inc., bet the Minister of South Australia he could build the biggest battery system in 100 days or he'd pay for it. A bodacious claim for the 100-megawatt project he completed with 40 days to spare[50] Musk is a man with big foresighted vision about the problems and the creative mega responses. Bodacious indeed.

- The organization, Well.org was created by Pedram Shojai, a teacher, acupuncturist, wellness consultant and filmmaker. In his work to revise old models stuck in the mode of scarcity and struggle, he sees a new framework worth holding onto—that of value and prosperity for all. Shojai showcased Thrive Market in his film "Prosperity," as an example of a successful Los Angeles 'For Benefit Business.'

- The Thrive mission is to bring healthy living into the world. For them, healthy living includes personal health as well as the health of the planet.

---

[49] "Residents, Cities Taking Charge of Protecting the Environment," Editorial, *Miami Herald,* November 22, 2017.
[50] Shannon Connellan, "Elon Musk had 100 days to build the world's biggest battery. He's done," Mashable.com November 22, 2017.

- The CEOs study the amounts of waste they create and aim for zero waste at their distribution centers.

- They revised how to repackage beans and now ship them in strong plastic bags rather than more energy-intensive cans.

- Co-owner Gunnar Lovelace was appalled to see the one step above slavery conditions for most coffee workers. Consequently, he engaged with Fair Trade growers to source Thrive's coffee beans.

- Food is another cog in the climate issue. Lovelace observes there is no way we can keep eating the amounts of meat we do.

- A comprehensive picture of their industry helps Lovelace to value regenerative agriculture. It is the best way to build topsoil, produce a higher quality of food, and enhance animal husbandry. At the same time, it generates more income for the company.

• The big-picture view is an important perspective in a food industry where, as Shojai said in his film, "the American taxpayer pays $25 million for junky, cheap food laced with chemicals and then these same taxpayers spend billions of dollars to care for sick people." This matters because we all vote with our money about the supply chain. It also matters because when people don't feel well and don't have energy, they put off considering these important aspects. The important piece to feeling well enough to make good decisions about your life and health and about the planet is—it and we are all connected. The world needs many of us operating with clear minds about our individual parts in degrading the environment with our food choices. Despite the fact that price, convenience, and values are often mixed up, now is the time to reorder these values in relation to long-term well-being.

- Lindsay Miles spoke at a TED talk about her heartfelt responses along her journey to using zero waste. This devoted recycler marveled "at how ridiculously over-packaged everything was in the supermarket." She wondered, "Why doesn't somebody do something about that?" Of course, her "recycling bin was always full;" so, she felt a little bit guilty about all that waste, "but my guilt just seems to melt away as soon as my recycling bin is collected," she noticed. Then Miles took on a month-long challenge to become plastic-free. Avoiding all single-use plastics amazed her with how many of these synthetic materials she uses.

- Zero waste living has improved Miles' life. She eats more real food, supports local independent businesses, has learned new skills and found ways to embrace creativity. She has connected with a community of like-minded people.

Most importantly, she realizes,
we can all do something about this problem.
We don't have to wait around for
"somebody to do something about it
because we all are somebody."

- Miles encourages people "not to get too hung up on perfection," but to do what they can, and to realize that actions are ripples which change an important story. "For too long we've believed companies telling us that convenience has to be disposable, but that's not true. Every time we shop, we can decide to perpetuate the problem or to be a part of the solution."[51] Once again, ordinary individuals truly are making a difference.

- The mayors of Los Angeles, Mexico City, London and Cape Town are among a group of 12 urban leaders vowing to buy only zero-emissions buses starting in 2025. They are making major portions of their metros fossil fuel-free by promoting walking, cycling, and public transportation, plus limiting the use of private vehicles.[52]

Not only do these personal, corporate and technological innovations help in the race against time, they also create new jobs for workers displaced as increasing numbers of businesses turn away from fossil fuels. New job creation generates more educational opportunities and more employment. Employed people pay taxes and buy from companies who also pay taxes. We all benefit. Plenty of people stand to gain from a world in the midst of a grand transition of pro-active changes.

---

[51] Katherine Martinko, "Don't Worry about Perfection when it Comes to Zero Waste," *Living/Green Home*, November 22, 2017
[52] Rachel Dovey, "12 Cities Plan for Emissions-Free Neighborhoods," *Next City*, October 23, 2017.

CHAPTER 7
Costs of Waiting

At exactly the time
when it has become clear that global warming
is in every sense a collective predicament,
humanity finds itself in the thrall
of a dominant culture
in which the idea of the collective has been exiled
from politics, economics and literature alike.
—Amitav Ghosh

Waiting and arguing about whether the climate is changing and who is responsible loses us time truly needed for activating ourselves and for finding resources. We need to get beyond the debate, and the hour is late. Coming to terms with the gravity of what climate change means requires both personal and collective participation.

The clock of climate change waits for no one
as it ticks well past quarter to midnight.

One great failure in the many years of an otherwise substantive environmental movement is the inability of environmentalists to entice and mobilize people in response to the prognostications for what is coming. We stubborn humans don't seem to stir until a rock hits us over the head. A favorable outcome of the massive storms of 2017 and yearly seasonal wildfires may be that they are frightening sufficiently to arouse people, whether rich or poor, educated or not, young or old. Sadly the poor, marginalized, infirm and older people will suffer most from the incessant delays; nonetheless, these events will affect everyone.

There are both social and economic costs to waiting. Senator Sheldon Whitehouse of Rhode Island, a persistent hero in consistently speaking on the Senate floor, said, "The social cost of carbon needs to be considered—to homeowners, families, business owners, and taxpayers—from drought-stricken farms and from raging wildfires, from floods and storm surges, from the effects of bark beetles killing pine forests and from fish disappearing from warming, acidifying waters. All of these harms carry real economic costs; so increasingly, federal courts, states, and big businesses are beginning to incorporate a social cost of carbon." This recognition is now valued as around $40 per ton of carbon pollution emitted.[53] Feedback loops are causing this number to be raised to $50 per ton of carbon.[54]

---

[53] The true cost of carbon pollution." Environmental Defense Fund edf.org.
[54] Chelsea Harvey, "Should the Social Cost of Carbon Be Higher?" *Scientific American*, November 22, 2017.

It helps to quantify costs for what is happening;
yet I am not so sure people can put a money value
on homes and memories lost,
on lives and families torn apart by storms,
on lives lost and injuries sustained.
Even so, $50 per ton emitted is a beginning.

On the other hand, Kerry Emanuel, an MIT Professor, climate scientist and leading researcher on tropical storms, does put a price figure on quantifiable losses. "Already, over the last four decades," he said, "hurricanes and cyclones globally have caused an average of $700 billion in damages annually since 1971."[55] Certainly insurance companies know these losses. Emmanuel cites population growth and the development of oceanfront property as contributing to a problem which is significantly growing larger as "the global population exposed to hurricanes has tripled since 1970."[56]

"While hurricanes, like earthquakes and volcanoes are part of nature," Emanuel continued, "what we're talking about are unnatural disasters, caused by structures built in places inherently vulnerable to such devastating forces. The physics behind the formation and growth of hurricanes indicates storm strength will continue to increase as the climate warms." …. "U.S. rainfall events as intense as what hurricanes Harvey and Florence produced, once had a 1% annual likelihood in the 1990s, (and) have already increased in likelihood to some 6% annually. By 2090

---

[55] David Chandler, "Kerry Emanuel: This year's hurricanes are a taste of the future," MIT News, September 21, 2017.
[56] ibid.

this figure may be 18%."[57] That's a lot of rain and certainly many more costs associated with floods and winds. Does your insurance company cover flood and wind damage?

Now let's look at other results from climate change, but first it may be time for another breathing opportunity. These breaks are here to emphasize how a regular practice of breathing empowers you because you are temporarily removing the obstacles to a greater spacious nature within.

What do you see outside that catches your attention?
Is the sky a clear blue? What birds do you see?
Is it raining cats and dogs?
That is beautiful too.
Breathe and settle into your moments of relaxation.

Busy life often obscures this realm of consciousness. Brief interludes, though, open you up to an ever present calm within you—a type of infinite freedom, contentment and happiness which is accessible even in the midst of challenging circumstances.

Contact your spacious nature often and enjoy.

---

[57] Ibid.

Okay, back to the challenges, especially with the health consequences of rising temperatures. Christian Clot is a French/Swiss explorer in great physical condition and with good equipment and knowledge for surviving harsh conditions. He is engaging in solo endurance trips to test the limits of human tolerance to heat. Writer Zoe Tabary surmises from conversations with Clot about his results, that, "If planet-warming emissions continue to rise at their current pace, three in four people in the world will face deadly heat by the turn of the century." This is a lot of people to be affected by heat.[58] Tabary continues her study with a report from Professor of Public Health Emily Y.Y. Chan from the Chinese University of Hong Kong. Chan says, "We found daily mortality increases by 1.8% for every degree above the threshold of 28.2° Celsius. Daily hospitalizations – for respiratory and infectious diseases, for example – increase by 4.5% for every degree above the threshold of 29° Celsius (84.2° Fahrenheit).... These figures suggest increasingly hot temperatures could leave health systems overwhelmed by surging demand."[59] Imagine the consequences for people in the 115° days common to places in Africa and more recently in Arizona?

Editors at The Lancet Journal reported from *The 2017 Lancet Countdown*, an international research group tracking the connections between public health and climate change: "In the past few years between 2000 and 2016, more about 125 million vulnerable adults over 65 years experienced heat waves each year, compared to about 19 million people per year in the

---

[58] Zoe Tabary, "Human frontiers: How much heat can the body and mind take?" *Thomson Reuters Foundation Newsletter.* https://www.nature.com/nclimate. September 22, 2017.
[59] ibid.

1990s."[60] Health consequences to increasing heat levels are huge. You probably know how bad it feels when the temperature rises too much. You don't feel like doing anything. Me either, but we are projected to get many more days of elevated temperatures. Ugly.

Breathe....

Another challenge is the refugee situation. A high likelihood exists that this planet in crisis will create an excess of thirty million refugees.[61] There is no system on Earth ready to handle this many displaced people. Already there are mounting issues with climate refugees who crowd into places unequipped for their onslaught. Time and dedication are penultimate to finding solutions which will work for all—for both natives who live there and for refugees who need a place to live. Certainly climate fugitives will appear.

With all these people moving around, moving our minds around is especially necessary, because these climate refugees are looking for safety *and an opportunity to contribute to their new homes*. Reframing the benefits they bring shows how they can make life better for the host country and for other new arrivals. Refugees bring with them intelligence, great courage, profound

---

[60]The Lancet Countdown. October 2017. www.thelancet.com
[61]Matthew Taylor. Climate change 'will create world's biggest refugee crisis. The Guardian.com November 2, 2017.

endurance and a first hand look at an unpleasant future. Their very presence is a warning sign urging us to figure out this new reality. I include this contentious issue because the enormity of our uncertain world brings a sharp focus to the need for ways to make it work for us all. Climate change is going to change us all in terms of how we think and what we do.

Look out your window…. And breathe….

Remember, one climate effect makes a difference to the others. Drought is a huge influence all over the world. It has been called one of the worst natural disasters partly because it can happen at any time, even in winter, and droughts may last for months or years. Surface or underground water receding when rain doesn't occur during long periods of time leads to drought conditions and the considerable damage resulting. Soils turned to crust substantially impact ecosystems, agriculture and the local economy as farmlands lie fallow and plants wither under relentless sun. People and animals must eat and drink, so as watering holes and rivers dry up, grazing animals and people migrate elsewhere toward water and food. *Dislocation becomes the rule.*

Drier droughts now extend farther and last much longer than in memorable past times. Central and western parts of the U.S. suffer especially, even as people in widespread areas of the country experience unusually dry conditions. Billions of dollars have been lost in damaged crops; as well, the health and safety of many is at risk. Warmer temperatures predicted by climate science will lead to increasingly drier and formerly unthinkable scenarios. One recent study by the National Center for Atmospheric Research shows large parts of the Western Hemisphere, Africa, and Asia being most threatened. A look at maps of Africa shows frightening amounts of increasingly brown rather than green areas fertile enough for food to grow. "One recent NASA study revealed that a drought which has been affecting the eastern Mediterranean Levant region since 1998 is likely the worst in the past 900 years."[62] People living in these regions are experiencing consequent hunger, dehydration and famine. They and animals are now searching for greener lands. Unrest often follows their migration, and wars can ignite over too many mouths vying for limited resources. Frightening indeed. Where will all those people get their food and where will they go when food is not available?

"Nearly 40% of the world's population of 7.6 billion people relies on agriculture."[63] Health and well-being become at risk for people, animals and communities who depend on these crops within the drought areas. This means all of us are threatened because most of our food supply is grown in essentially an irrigated desert in California and in the southwest. Food costs rise along with food shortages when farmers can't grow the crops demanded. Even for the lucky ones who live in the U.S. where other sources for food are available, food shortages apply to all of us wanting the

---

[62] Op. cit. The Lancet.
[63] Ibid.

food choices on which we've come to depend for our daily nourishment.

Severe droughts lasting years have many effects. Winds cause dry land to blow away and erode the soil quality. Remember the *Grapes of Wrath* John Steinbeck wrote about with its dust bowls, dust storms and refugees moving west? Water levels fall and harsh winds dry out skin. Dry cracked earth becomes rock like and ungrowable. Constantly howling winds spook people. Trees die and animals forage further. To put it mildly, life in the midst of a severe drought seems highly uncomfortable.

Drought brings into question the viability of continuing to live in places once considered desert. Many parts of California, Arizona and the Southwest are examples of former deserts irrigated and brought to life. These precarious water supplies are once again dwindling even at the same time as more people move to escape northern winters. A dystopian novel by Paolo Bacigalupi, *The Water Knife*, describes unhappy results of not paying attention to these factors in time when we are able to do so. The novel sets itself in an Arizona upset by lack of water for most of its residents. The wealthy people live comfortably in self-contained dwellings rising many stories above the desert. These buildings are complex, technological machines which provide everything the inhabitants need, including growing their food, insulating them from heat and protecting against marauders. Life for most of the other people outside these castles is dry, dangerous and lacking in creature comforts.

Time to stop and breathe again....

You are here right now, sitting in your chair and reading a book.
Breathe and feel your feet on the ground....

Increasing numbers of wildfires are another happenstance from climate change. Droughts dry out the land, kill plant life and create tinderbox conditions where dead trees and vegetation become excellent fodder for large destructive fires. Wildfires are horrible events which never become commonplace, yet we repeatedly see infernos on television. Because of rising temperatures, shorter winters, and longer summers, the western U.S. wildfire frequency has increased by 556% since the 1970's and 80's.[64] Damaging wildfires have occurred in recent years in California, Colorado, Arizona, Oregon, Washington state, Montana and New Mexico. It's as if the entire west is on fire. The fires last longer, happen more often and are more extensive than ever. Less predictable rains and erratic winds leave the conflagrations harder to stop once they begin. These unstoppable fires are unbelievably expensive to manage. Think Sonoma, Santa Rosa, Los Angeles, Montana. People, animals, homes and businesses wiped out. Serious stuff.

---

[64] "Wildfires in West have gotten bigger, more frequent and longer since the 1980s," *The Conversation*, May 23, 2016

Getting back to food. There are many possible responses to the dilemma with what will we eat in a constrained future. Every region experiencing the effect of a changing climate will witness and feel the effects of altered food production. Farmers are already having to learn to grow in harsher conditions. They are changing what and how they grow vegetables and how they raise livestock. There will probably be disconnects in availability of what we commonly expect, for this type of learning doesn't happen overnight. Farming involves much experiment-ation and waiting, then more trials to get to the right mix of ingredients and weather. We will all be part of a learning curve.

The oceans are changing too. According to important studies conducted by biologist Rebecca Asch on seasonal cycles in relation to weather and climate, the Pacific Islands region is growing warmer, with less oxygen and more acid in the waters. Species are sensitive to these changes and so Asch foresees less plankton available for larger fishes to eat. She "found that local extinction of marine species exceeds 50% of current biodiversity levels across many regions and at times reached levels over 80%."[65] Asch calls this a worst case scenario which could be prevented by action now.

"Additional warming will push ocean temperature beyond conditions organisms have not experienced since geological time periods in this region,"[66] co-author Gabriel Reygondeau, Nereus Fellow at the University of British Columbia, said in a statement,

---

[65] "Climate change could kill 50-80% of Pacific fish species:A conversation with Rebecca Asch, *RadioNZ,* November 22, 2017.
[66] Ian Johnston, "More than Seven Hundred Species Facing Extinction are Being Hit by Climate Change," *The Independent,* February 14, 2017.

"Since no organisms living in the ocean today could have time to adapt to these warmer conditions, many will either go extinct or migrate away from the western Pacific, leaving this area with much lower biodiversity."[67] *These figures don't have to be inevitable.*

And then there's the earth's mantle of ice. Land ice all over the world is melting much faster than ever imagined. Glaciers in the Himalayas, Chile, Glacier National Park, Greenland, and everywhere. Once again the extremely precise computer projections were unable to completely foresee the results of these amounts of cascading events. Scientists knew concurrent alterations would come about when warmer air currents blew north, but back in the seventies and eighties they could not anticipate the degree of warming or the amounts of ice melt. Land ice melting means higher sea levels happening sooner than expected. Higher sea levels earlier than we thought can and will press on us to get moving. Almost every major city on all the coasts in the world lies within distance of those rising waters. Virtually every military installation was built on coastlines. These are major snags to continuing on with life as usual.

Icebergs break off every day. Less ice decreases their heat reflecting powers. Sea waters surge into where ice was once intact and then rushing waters carve out channels and diminish the size of the remaining icebergs, which then become more vulnerable to collapse. All this frozen water is supposed to be part of the earth's natural cooling system, which provides balance to the heat in

---

[67] Gabriel Reygondeau. "Pacific Island countries could lose 50-80% of fish in local waters under climate change." Nereus Program News Highlights. 11/15/17.

other areas. At this point we have intensifying heat everywhere else on the planet and less ice for balance. Not good.

Animals in the wild are suffering too. "More than Seven Hundred Species Facing Extinction are Being Hit by Climate Change" is the title of a report by Ian Johnston in *The Independent*.[68] The no-longer-stable climate is affecting mammals and birds as they arrive earlier to find off-kilter springtimes which disrupt their nesting patterns, schedules, and feedings. I saw this sad nuance recently during an extended warm spell in February, when a flock of robins arrived in Rhode Island, days before March roared in with bitter temperatures and four weekly snowstorms of 8-18" each. Warmer temperatures are changing the geographic ranges for birds, too. They fly farther for what they need. Insects and even trees are migrating north to cooler climes.

Changing weather patterns mean winter ice storms are moving to where once, early snow reigned supreme for skiers and ski areas, who will no longer be happy.

Forests are experiencing massive die-offs. Oliver Milman and Alan Yuhas chronicled some of this destruction in their *Guardian* newspaper report about the stress on millions of trees across the country dying from drought, disease, insects and wildfire.[69] You have probably noticed this too. I have seen pine bark beetles lay waste to mountainsides in North Carolina and I've seen hills of brown trees in California. The mysterious "O hi" disease, spread by the wings of beetle borers, may precipitate the loss of native

---

[68] Op cit. Johnston.
[69] Milman and Yuhas, "An American Tragedy: Why are Millions of Trees Dying?" *The Guardian*, September 19, 2017.

forests in Hawaii. Sudden oak disease is prevalent and is devastating oak trees in northern California. Sixty-six million trees have died in the Sierra Nevadas since 2010. This really matters because the essential role of trees—to shelter ecosystems and clean water, to lock in carbon—is being undermined by the massive die-offs. Trees hold mountains together by preventing erosion, rock slides and mudslides. Five years of drought and wildfires in the West have weakened trees so that insects can take over. The outbreak of these beetle and disease infestations is ten times greater than normal. Deaths of more trees change habitats for animals who count on their shelter and nutrients. These creatures must move on. They then become more climate refugees crowding into someone else's ecosystem. The *Guardian* article calls these changes partially due to climate change and partly due to imported invasive plants. Both of these are man-made invasions. So sad....

National security is being affected by climate change as well, despite the results of a 2017 Pew Research poll showing only 56% of Americans recognize climate change as a national security threat. Rear Admiral David Titley, USN (Ret.), Advisory Board, The Center for Climate and Security, reports that the Department of Defense (DOD) must be ready and able to maintain an effective and efficient military in regard to identifying and assessing effects and risks of climate change on the DOD mission, in order for them to build resilience.[70]

---

[70] David Titley, "New Dept. of Defense Directive on Climate and Security," The Center for Climate and Security, January 20, 2016.

The Intergovernmental Panel on Climate Change (IPCC) report adds to the concern with its statement that, "impacts of climate-related extremes include alteration of ecosystems, disruption of food production and water supply, damage to infrastructure and settlements, increased violent conflict, morbidity and mortality, and consequences for mental health and human well-being. For countries *at all levels of development* (my emphasis), these impacts are consistent with a significant lack of preparedness for current climate variability in some sectors." Indeed a concern. We all are vulnerable—and this is a new feeling for many of us in the U.S. where bombs have never fallen and where we have been protected from conflict by vast ocean distances.

No one is safe anymore from the many ways in which climate change will alter the course of our lives—*unless we get active now.* Consider this option ... your behaviors in support of the natural world will literally preserve the best of what we experience in life. On top of this, your responses will definitely enhance our common economic benefits, because a heightened level of change means plenty of new occasions for finding meaningful work.

Security experts are not so naive to ignore the fact of most of our military base locations are along coastlines. Norfolk, Virginia is in the process of shoring up its massive military base because it experiences coastal flooding twice a day at each high tide. That is—high tide everyday, not once in a while. Twice a day. A recent study from the Union of Concerned Scientists found a 3' sea level rise would threaten 128 coastal military installations in the U.S.

alone.[71] *This is a problem.* In 2017 we witnessed the total destruction of Barbuda in the Caribbean Sea after Hurricane Irma. We also stood in awe of the 33 trillion gallons of water dumped on Houston, and we saw the decimation of Puerto Rico's electrical system, homes, businesses, and lives. National security specialists factor these happenings and research in conjunction with the damaging flooding around the world. These experts take into account the security threats in places like Sierra Leone, Bangladesh and Latin America, to name a few recently inundated places.

Water-borne diseases and insects accompany flood waters and exacerbate the distress for newly flooded-out and homeless people. Projections suggest sea level rises will affect millions of people across the country and around the planet. Great movements of these people as they flee danger zones destabilizes local and national governments. In response, the current defense secretary James Mattis stated, "Climate change is impacting stability in areas of the world where our troops are operating today."[72] The military attends closely to currents of people flowing away from disasters. Frightened people can lead to conflicts in efforts to feed and shelter their families. Remember the chaos in New Orleans after Katrina?

Erratic climates are taxing the armed forces, which are stressed in plenty of other ways. They must respond in the form of humanitarian relief. Increases are needed for military monitoring of sea lanes as they expand and move around the freed-up ice

---

[71] Andrew Revkin. "Trump's Defense Secretary Cites Climate Change as National Security Challenge." Pro Publica. 3/14/17.
[72] "The US Military on the Front Lines of Rising Seas," *Union of Concerned Scientists*, 2016.

masses in the Arctic. Consequently, the numbers of troops used for relief and for monitoring larger expanses of ocean affect operational readiness in other areas. As vast as our military is, there is only so much of it to spread around the whole earth. A cause for concern amongst military minds.

Leaving the military aspect behind, equity looms large. "Climate change is the biggest ethical, moral and spiritual challenge of our day," according to Joan Brown, Executive Director of the New Mexico Interfaith Power & Light.[73] Equity for all reframes the whole climate change issue into one of inclusion for most of the earth's seven and a half billion people, who have little capacity to decrease their carbon emissions. These people already don't use much energy in their daily lives. We in the wealthy world do use great quantities of energy and often don't even recognize the privilege of our gift. People who live far away suffer and are unseen by those of us who continue on with our wastefulness.

Kevin Anderson, the climate science theorist from the UK, suggests using equity as a baseline approach to energy usage. Anderson says the concept of equity presents a huge opportunity for great and good change. We can embrace long-term goals for participating in the efforts toward climate actions and then in evaluating progress along the way. He sees this style of change as a good model for some people to be catalysts in stepping away from an out-of-date system. The beauty of changing in this way is that projected changes can be mapped backward to identify necessary preconditions. Then, this information will guide the

---

[73] Sarah Tory, "Religious communities are taking on climate change," *High Country News,* September 18, 2017.

steps forward. The meat of the issue is, "discussing the facts of climate change isn't enough. That's where religion comes in. At a certain point, you have to talk about the consequences and past that, it becomes a conversation about morality," said David Radcliffe, director of the New Community Project in Vermont.[74] Even without religion factoring in, people are beginning to realize it feels deeply wrong to be destroying our habitat in ways which will create suffering for future generations. Changing the old mindset is where it's at; and it feels gratifying to come to these conclusions.

We're talking about equity, yet climate change also has to do with health. Untold numbers of people living near refineries and chemical plants suffer the unseen health consequences of polluted air and unsavory drinking water, from oil and pipeline spills, from railroad cars and methane tanks exploding. It isn't funny to know the sellers of these tanks told us how safe they were. Residents living near such perils are often lower income people who lack choice about housing locations. No one else wants to live near hazards, so the land around dangerous sites becomes affordable and often people don't know what nearby could harm them. They unknowingly move in and sometime down the road, their health is affected. Days at work or in school are lost because their fitness is compromised with breathing problems and other pollution-related diseases. Needed money goes down the drain after they lose their work and the costs of being sick mount up. Lower income people don't have a safety net of extra funds, nor do they have options. Their futures become even more precarious. This is not equitable.

---

[74] https://www.newcommunityproject.org.

All this information is a lot to take in; so let's take another break.

Time to breathe again and remember the goodness inside you.
Take three breaths deep into your belly.
Effortlessly and easily.
May every breath remind you
of the whole beautiful being you are.
Let every inhalation bring in the fragrance of life.

***

Now for a look at GOOD NEWS…. Finally….

More than 1,400 U.S. cities, states and businesses vowed to meet the Paris Climate agreements. Rather than a head-in-the-sand approach, this significant number of U.S. citizens recognizes the essential need for action.

The New Climate Institute and the nonprofit organization called The Climate Group analyzed carbon-reduction commitments from 22 states, 54 cities, and 250 U.S. companies. The two organizations projected, "if these groups follow through, U.S. carbon emissions in 2025 will be 12-14% lower than the 2005 level. States provided more than two-thirds of the emissions reductions; companies (except for electric utilities) were also big reducers, many of which committed to significantly lower emissions by converting to renewable energy."[75] Together we can do this. This degree of willpower will help us stop further carbon emissions.

The US Climate alliance found,
"states didn't have to make economic sacrifices
to pursue climate action plans;
in actuality, the economies of states
within the U.S. Climate Alliance
grew faster than those in the rest of the country." [76]

This is good news indeed, news to hold onto as you survey the rest of what you read. Matter of fact, it's probably good to return to these messages over and over, to reassure yourself that, indeed, climate sense is crucial and that we together can make meaningful progress. After this cursory look at what's up with climate change, from now on—*whoopee!*—we'll look at positive constructive responses and what you can do now. Time for hope and possibility—time for inspiration.

I have a little different definition of evil than most people.
When you have the opportunity and the ability to do good
and you do nothing, that's evil.
Evil doesn't always have to be an overt act.
It can be merely the absence of good. The cure is action.
—Yvon Chouinard
Founder of the outdoor gear company Patagonia

---

[75]US Climate Alliance & The Climate Group report, September 13, 2017
[76]US Climate Alliance Fact Sheet. 2018.

CHAPTER 8
What's Positive Here?

People are inherently good
Our planet is in trouble
Business "as usual" is making it worse and...
TOGETHER we can fix it.
—Dr. Pedram Shojai

Positive things are happening much more than we know, and we can contribute to this trend. *Look for encouraging news.* We live in indescribably unsettling times, and still within this mix is abundant positive news. Unfortunately, 'what doesn't bleed doesn't sell,' so we don't hear much of the constructive good which happens all the time. Dr. Pedram Shojai, creator of the film "Prosperity," footnoted in Chapter 1, agrees about the good happening all around us, yet as he says, "we don't even have eyes to see it!" Our eyes need to widen, so we can receive and then relay the good news as social media begins to deliver it. Positive happenings encourage us when all seems dark. The mechanisms for sharing are available.

Collaborate. Plenty of people recognize the climate issues and are inventing ways to solve problems. Young people are speaking up about the world they are to inherit. As it happens, a group of these young people are suing corporations for knowingly blocking research and information and especially for denying that climate change even exists. Other people gather in groups, on their own, without government leadership, to figure out ways to move forward. Together we are progressing. And this is fitting because evolutionary biology tells us that collaboration is every bit as important as competition.

Talk about it. I can't emphasize enough how great is the urgency to meaningfully address climate change. I know I repeat myself about the clarion call, but here's a radical take on how to respond—talk about climate change. People don't seem to want to talk about it, even though it is monumentally consequential to all our lives. Not talking about climate change is a dilemma. Here's a solution for how to begin these conversations: a positive response to a changing climate is the lead-in with which each of us can begin. This one step of talking about climate change is immensely important. Pulling these discussions out of the dark closet to where we can talk about them allows us to move forward. We must talk about the problems and our fears before we can move ahead. We must learn from each other. But first, an edifying side note may help these exchanges.

Bringing climate change home to our hearts is pivotal. The conversation allows us to feel the concerns about how it impacts us, our friends and families. Feeling the feelings is a huge step.

The discussions and the emotions brought up may be scary. However, becoming aware of them does not sentence us to be frozen and flustered forever. *We can and do move through uncomfortable feelings all the time.* Truly experiencing the responses moves us to the other side where it is possible to act upon them.

Yes, the whole business is most depressing; nonetheless, change comes about through genuinely becoming aware of the dilemma. You know it, you see it, you feel it. Otherwise we simply observe rather than take our place in history. Truly engaging with the stressful emotions around this enormous conundrum is the key to moving forward—to feeling liberated and to leaving behind enslavement by fear.

Climate change conversations begin most comfortably when you can share things to do now. I feel better when I can begin to act on what feels so very large. I see myself more constructively because there is some way to play a part. Alone and with no encouragement I may feel depressed, overwhelmed and without a clue. The main point is that, side by side, our collective wisdom empowers us all. We simply begin with what we are good at— speaking with others.

Let's look now at a few helpful ventures around the world. These describe a world which recognizes the problem. Perhaps what they do will facilitate your next steps. Perhaps you will feel as if together we all are making a difference.

Pedram's movie, "Prosperity," portrays successful companies solving local and global problems by way of capitalism. These companies have moved well beyond the debate to see an opportunity for business within the scenario of adapting to a climate in the midst of change. For example, the Global Building Council finds 40% of energy use arises from buildings themselves, which waste heat and air conditioning. Engineering and new product solutions are resolving such inefficiency. Thus New York, with its unique density and 80% energy wastage, has decided to construct nearly all new buildings as green. Efficient building does not cost more; as a matter of fact, the savings over lengthy stretches of time are significant. Long-term thinking is simply smart business strategy. Paul Gilding, author of *The Great Disruption,* emphasizes this fact with the assertion that there are no serious people in the business community who don't believe that serious changes are coming. Businesses who understand this approach are moving ahead of more short-sighted competitors.

All of our financial contributions can assist with the climate dilemma. Banking with a conscience, that is, investing for benefit rather than for profit only, is a strong alternative for placing your money. Safe ethically-minded banks exist, even if they require some searching to find what you trust. Conscious capitalism and triple bottom line investing for people, planet and profit is outperforming peer companies whose primary goal is making money. Banking and investing for the next quarter only does not help anyone except the short-term investors who will also have to survive long-lasting climate changes.

A new sense of stakeholder ownership is a second way to make a difference with your presence and with your money. The stakeholder concept addresses morals and values, such that everyone matters and everyone benefits. Those who benefit include customers, the environment, workers, shareholders, community and company. This perspective is brewing now even though we don't often hear about it. You are now aware, so search it out if this appeals to you. The film "Prosperity" gives you resources.

When you choose where to spend your money beyond banking and finance you become a stakeholder in those companies. There is a bit more work to figuring out where a product comes from and what it supports, but ultimately your efforts are worth it. Buying what you want to see more of in the world supports good companies which are making a difference.

The third financial contribution in how you spend your money is to think about these questions—do I need this shirt, this car, that appliance, whatever? Where was this product built and at whose cost? What distances did it travel to meet your whims? Is this product a whim or a need for me? Think avocados and peaches in winter. Think Chilean raspberries. All delicious, and I love them as much as the next person; even so, they come at a great carbon expense to the world. It takes energy to transport goods around the world. We've certainly become used to what once were luxuries indeed. In this climate-centric world, these out of season wonders have turned into carbon luxuries; so, the question becomes, is this purchase making the world a better place, or is it making it worse?

The fourth economic choice is a bit more drastic. You can choose to work for companies better aligned with your values. They exist; you only have to seek them out. Find a company you respect and ask about hiring. You may be surprised at their response. Good companies are looking for people whose values align with theirs.

A fifth financial contribution to a healthier world is to assess and reorder your retirement accounts so they make a positive impact. Ask the company where you work to set up separate accounts which allow you to invest as you choose. Then you no longer place your money with people whose values do not align with your own.

Bottom line: we all need to think differently.
Your voice matters.

Back to the good news now; here are some innovative companies. *PowerDocks* in Rhode Island is creating autonomous renewable energy stations to charge boats and gear right in their waterway locations, whether it be in the ocean or on marina slips. These docks draw on battery-stored energy to charge and power pleasure boats, oceanographic research, military operations and commercial applications such as aquaculture. The company provides a meaningful benefit by reducing the vast amounts of polluting gasoline used in boating. Owner Anthony Baro says marinas usually operate at 80-85% capacity, so *PowerDocks* will increase profitability for the marinas by repurposing empty slips into sun-powered generating facilities. Even though this is a very coastal-specific idea, let yourself imagine what creative things are possible wherever you live.

BBOXX in London manufactures, installs, and affordably loans out sturdy, hyper-efficient solar-powered chargers. In four years, they have brought power to 130,000 homes and businesses in 35 countries. By 2020, they anticipate more than a million homes and businesses energized by BBOXX. The company relies on a "pay as you go" system to bring off-grid energy to some 1.2 billion people in developing countries around the world, where this 16% of the global population does not have access to energy.[77] Pay as you go is a brilliant and affordable idea, for each family pays when they need power. Before the advent of these options, energizing an entire country was a major roadblock.

Here is an example of people joining together to solve a problem. Architects, urban planners, environmentalists and others gathered in a low-income Canal neighborhood in San Rafael, California to contemplate ways to keep increasingly rising waves in the bay from overrunning land. The entire community is happy to be working together with poor neighborhoods, and it also recognizes a broader benefit of tackling the rising sea levels together. These rising waters eventually will "affect downtown as well as the Transit Center," they say as they acknowledge, "we are in this together."[78] These people chose hope embodied in action as the seas continue to rise.

We *are* in this together, and our collective minds can solve what individual wits cannot yet see. Other companies are joining their intellectual capabilities with others. In the United Kingdom,

---

[77] Rachel Nuwer, "Rural Rwanda is Home to a Pioneering New Solar Power Idea," *BBC Future Now*, October 9, 2017.
[78] Mark Prado, "Marin thinkers join effort to tackle sea-level rise," *Marin Independent Journal*, October 5, 2017.

automobile maker Nissan and energy supplier Ovo are pioneering a plan to offer "vehicle-to-grid" services to buyers of the Japanese carmaker's newest model, "Leaf," an innovative electric car. Ovo will install a special charger and then pay electric car owners who allow the energy company to utilize the car batteries when the car is not being driven. Car owners determine a minimum amount of charge needed to drive the next day and then Ovo automatically uses the battery's excess electricity, topping it off in low-cost, off-peak times, and then selling it for about four times as much to power companies who need it at peak energy use hours.

The Leaf/Ovo plan intends to both increase sales of cleaner vehicles and to help power grids manage an anticipated increased amount of fluctuating green energy. This is a transformational future where flexible arrangements between power grid managers and millions of electric cars replace costly grid upgrades and new power stations needing to be built.[79] People are thinking hard about the need to build new power plants which require fossil fuel energy for the life of those plants. So far we've seen several options to accomplish this—Canada's tons of available hydroelectric power, the Tesla PowerWall, and now the Leaf/Ovo collaboration.

How we eat is such a huge contributor to a warming climate. There are many positive happenings in the food realm. Robin Scher wrote *Why Plant Based Shrimp is the Next Veggie Burger,* an article about the food company New Wave which is creating a plant and algae-based shrimp. The product tastes and looks like

---

[79] Adam Vaughan, "Electric car owners can drive for free by letting energy firms use battery," *The Guardian*, October 2, 2017.

real shrimp, yet it has no harmful chemicals or pollutants. Another bonus is that this pseudo-shrimp production does not ruin the mangrove forests crucial to the livelihood of coastal peoples as does conventional shrimp farming. Apparently, this shrimp looks good, tastes good, and is ready to market.[80] This benefit will be huge, for vast amounts of shrimp are continually consumed. Let's hope this new version does taste really good.

Food waste is another piece in the spectrum of possible food industry interventions. Much of the food that cycles from farm to restaurants, schools, institutions and to your plate goes unused. Huge quantities of food grown ends up wasted and in landfills, some 500,000 tons in the small state of Connecticut alone. Quantum Biopower is a company there which is making electricity from 40,000 tons of food waste generated by local businesses per year. This electricity alone is enough to power one thousand homes. Imagine what is possible if, after giving food away and composting residuals, we put even more food waste to better use.

Money saved is most decidedly a driver for making changes, which benefit the business owner and the environment. A Midwestern poultry farmer figured a way to cut his heating bills in half.[81] Bill Bevans installed in his barns a waste-heat recovery system developed by a researcher at the University of Missouri-Columbia. The heat-exchange technique transfers warm exhaust air from the poultry house to the fresh cold air entering. "Reduced fuel use by

---

[80] Robin Scher, "Why Plant-based Shrimp is the Next Veggie Burger," *Alternet,* October 18, 2017.
[81] Karen Uhlenhuth, "Midwestern poultry farmers cut bills in half with new heating system," *Midwest Energy News*, October 12, 2017.

50% in thousands of barns has tremendous benefit as far as carbon reduction," Bevans said about his barns. Each barn uses 25 times more energy than a single-family house. Chickens love this change because they thrive on the reduced humidity in the houses. Thriving birds lead to healthier chickens needing fewer antibiotics. This creates another win-win all around because healthier birds and less use of antibiotics improve our health.

Albert Straus is another farmer solving a problem. His organic dairy farm in Marin County, California, produces tons of cow manure. He figured out how to use the cow waste to generate electricity and then built an electric truck powered by that electricity to feed his cows. He reduces methane emissions and uses the potent greenhouse gas to power his whole farm. Talk about a virtuous cycle.

The investment firm Vanguard is also using the money-saved angle in its approach to corporations. Rob Main with the Investment Stewardship division at Vanguard said in the film "Prosperity" that, "For many companies across sectors like the materials sector, the energy sector, the industrial sector, the topic of climate risk is going to be very relevant.... We have a starting point of believing that well-governed companies will be better performers long term." Being proactive around these risks helps Vanguard choose the least risky investments for their clients.

Part of the reason for sharing these positive stories is—if these people, towns and companies can make such substantial changes in how they go about their lives and businesses, *so can we*. They inspire us to a better future. Also, what I have seen of pioneers who transition away from fossil fuels is singing, dancing, gardening and play. There is more walking and more outdoor exercise and greater health. People who are out in nature experience happiness. This is a different take on the cli-fi disaster-only model presented to us. The crux of peaceful change is to get busy now.

Working together is a positive breakthrough with long roots,
from faraway places and from nature.
Nonetheless, a collective mentality of working
for the good of all contrasts greatly
with the more solo and competitive ways
we modern folks have come to know.
The author Amitav Ghosh suggests,
"Climate change challenges our central tenet of freedom
without non-human constraints."[82]

Certain people, who often live outside the United States, and who truly understand the dire needs, are working together to step up with solutions. Consequently, they are funding the most audacious ideas about technology and climate change. We can learn from these forerunners as well as from the bees and ants about how each category of their social structure works together to support the whole community. Bees forage for and bring back nectar, protect the hive, and serve more than themselves. Have you noticed how ants carry huge weights on their backs and how other ants help them? Or how they create big swarms to bring back food to their nests? Insects are not the only ones with a

---

[82] Amitav Ghosh. The Great Derangement. Climate Change and the Unthinkable. University of Chicago Press. 2016.

collective intent; ancient tribes worked together because they had to. Some of us, especially those people in Asia, also have long histories of collaborating. The continent has much to lose and billions of lives at risk from rising seas and melting glaciers. Yet the sheer numbers of people in Asia who are modernizing make this continent a major driver of climate change. People in the Asian countries absolutely need to work together. How they respond will teach others of us in the western world. It is time we all begin to trust in "hive" mentality again—to work collectively on the biggest projects of our lives.

Urgency moves climate change to the forefront of our imaginations and well beyond an *individual* problem. Urgency becomes *our* opportunity to work and play together with the crisis at hand. You don't have to change the whole world to expand the hive concept to a human scale. As the filmmaker Pedram Shojai said in "Prosperity", "What if you are sick and tired of being told what to do? What if you can solve that problem?" The answer is to step out of the trance of helplessness which society has fallen into. This trance mindset gets in the way of abundant thinking— we are intelligent and creative enough to imagine a positive future. Shojai again in the film: "The world starts to change when you think of abundance and possibilities rather than scarcity and lack of instant solutions. What matters is what do I want this world to look like." Strangely enough, with this new mindset, waiting for the government to lead us becomes irrelevant.

Nonetheless, political action is probably the best motivator for people as it brings the issue into more people's awareness. Soooo....

Simply launch yourself where you are,
with what you see in front of you
and what you really care about.
Take information and actionable intelligence
about what you can do
and begin right now, right where you are.
Each constructive change helps and inspires others
around the world
to find more and better solutions.

As it turns out, abundance is a new definition of global prosperity. This is a profoundly new way to look at dilemmas—to step out of hopelessness and wait for someone else to fix it—to see a rapidly evolving world full of new companies and fast-moving technology. New mindsets are disrupting the old ways. The passive trajectory of humanity changes when people yearn for constructive solutions to what were seen as unsolvable problems. Seeing these innovations and progress helps us override old and limiting identities. What we catch sight of urges us to jump off the curb of stasis so we move into a future of exciting potential.

But how does this revised mindset come about? Turns out it is really quite simple. Naveen Jain is a successful entrepreneur and visionary thinker who, in the film "Prosperity" posits asking ourselves these questions, "What would you die for and live for? What if you had one year to live? What if you already had enough money?" Jain suggests beginning with your desired purpose and going from there. Purpose is what brings fulfilling happiness—not things, houses, cars. Finding true purpose motivates going after this deeper level of fulfillment. This is inspiration in action. Each person on this earth needs this from you.

Now is the perfect time to take a few moments
to breathe and to write about these questions.

When you're surrounded by people
who share a passionate commitment
around a common purpose,
anything is possible.
—Howard Shultz
businessman

CHAPTER 9
Big Plans for Action Now

Never doubt that a small group of
thoughtful, committed citizens
can change the world;
indeed, it's the only thing that ever has.
—Margaret Mead

This Earth crisis with one horrible prediction after the other, all competing for attention, can put a person into apocalyptic shock. Stop—hit the pause button on this thought: What if, together, we could imagine finding ways to change the trajectory of climate decline? What if we could imagine discovering projects now invisible, but ones which could show up when lots of people choose to work for meaningful change? What if we could simply hold the door of possibility open for this? What if....

Some people may call this fanciful wishing. Truthfully, regardless of its "fanciful" thinking, no one really knows what lies in our future. The great unknown in all the figures and projections is the *human element* of a cooperative focus. Bouncing around ideas can stimulate new thoughts, which may turn out to be particularly valuable approaches. Can we choose to hold this promise? I believe if enough of us choose to join together, we can change the course on climate change. The magic in this is that by doing so we attract more and more people who contribute their efforts to this inspiring cause. These people simultaneously attract others. Will you help to hold onto this hopeful vision?

You may feel climate change is too big, and wonder what difference one person can make, and "where can I begin anyway?" Notwithstanding the daunting nature of the whole world as we know it being radically altered, there is much we can do. There are many people with whom we can speak. Only six degrees of separation removes people from others and from influential people who can persuade even more people. Six degrees is all that keeps us apart us from what we might want to know. Holding out hope and intention for the best possible outcomes will happen when we call upon our shared consciousness and for our mutual connections to arise. This stance invigorates me as it fills me with passion. Can you sense this growing in yourself also?

While this thought percolates within you, let's look at what you can do to find willing partners in the efforts to ameliorate climate change. Most of us are very good at talking, so it's an easy step to begin conversations about the changing climate with your friends, families, town councils and fellow employees. Entice them with the good things going on. Involve them by asking about their personal changes and what they are noticing. The cornerstone to these conversations is to grasp the link between our actions and outcomes. Understanding how far away we have come from being in greater harmony with the earth can be a game of discovery. As you talk together, share what is possible. Explain the pressing need for each of us to be agents of change. Talk. Spreading the word is an ongoing constructive contribution which matters so much. These are personal conversations and they are political, for looking into what individuals and communities can control empowers people to know they can do something that matters. Your conversations are enticing people to become part of the positive.

Getting started straight away matters, and is especially important with our concurrent lack of a government rally and focused leadership. We individuals are the leaders who can press on the state and town levels. The Climate Mobilization (TCM) is a group calling for massive scale efforts—a "Moonshot" approach, or as in the Marshall Plan, which helped rebuild Europe after the World War II devastation. It's true such mobilizations galvanize people and corporations to progress quickly. This level of support and encouragement is truly what is needed; however, given the head-in-the-sand tone of the day, the progression of a seriously altered climate cannot wait for a government change of mind amid the endless political debates. In the absence of such overriding leadership, individuals who understand can accomplish much by stepping up to the challenges. When people begin to change at this moment in time, large scale efforts will follow as a consensus of people demands great endeavors.

Ezra Silk of TCM describes the situation this way, "We face a series of time sensitive existential emergencies which can only be overcome successfully with a drastic transformation of the entire economy ... accomplished at wartime speed ... The urgency in the current trajectory of rising temperatures, carbon dioxide levels and intensifying storms calls for a large-scale mobilization to restore the Earth—a Victory Plan to reach net zero greenhouse gas emissions in less than 10 years."[83]

Massive plans are thought to be the only and best way to stabilize the climate change needle, and yet... TEN YEARS to massively transform all areas of life seems exceptionally ambitious. Nonetheless, TCM and others maintain that every available tool must be used as quickly as possible to remove excess carbon from the atmosphere, and "to restore a safe and stable climate which supports the continuation of an organized human "community." TCM envisions a powerful Mobilization Board aligned with the Department of Defense and with the Federal Reserve Commission to generate financing and labor for a spectrum of components called for in relation to transportation, agriculture and a transformed food system, accelerated renewable energy produc- tion, rationing of greenhouse gas emissions, and much more.

Once again though, despite the critical moment and the enor- mous issues, I struggle with the extended debate and time spent before this sweeping level of engagement will be enacted. I hope TCM succeeds with its fine proposals, and in the meantime, we can get going. More immediate and feasible undertakings are called for while bold ideas are being put into place. Once the

---

[83] Ezra Silk, The Climate Mobilization Victory Plan, page 10. The Climate Mobilization.org.

gravity of our shared situation sinks in, we each will have a hard time sitting still waiting. We will want to get going on what works. But first, we must come to grips with a sense of the calamity happening all over the world, way beyond our own backyards.

The group, Civic Alliance for a Cooler Rhode Island (CACRI)[84] developed an actionable plan ready for immediate use. The framers of this strategy intend that people change eating, traveling, land use habits, as well as other aspects of how we live—fundamentally, to use fewer fossil fuels. *Leave them in the ground* is essentially the political motto of their program which calls on you to drive less and walk instead, bike where you can, share rides on the way to work, and use public transit when possible. In short, the plan calls on you, and shows you how to reduce electricity use by converting vehicles, heating systems and eventually all energy needs away from fossil fuels. The goal is for electricity to be powered by renewable energies which are not depleted as they are used, but are generated over and again. Local governments can make use of this good news, for such proactive habit changes will also strengthen the economy and enhance communities. Creative solutions which work now are a proven alternative to waiting for disasters to destroy the patterns of life we have come to count upon every day.

While the CACRI plan will not automatically muster a massive mobilization, *it does offer people strategies to begin today* and is a foundation for political outreach. It counts on people's efforts growing as does a snowball rolling downhill. The first step really matters, for quite simply, when more people join in, the effect is exponential. One: we make changes, two: we tell others, three:

---

[84] CACRI.org.

they listen, and four: rinse and repeat. We grow in numbers, unshackle ourselves, and strengthen in resolve.

Both the individual plans of CACRI and the massive TCM plans have merit and a place in a progression toward a newfound, healthier future. Everyone can educate themselves into habits of doing more and more to interrupt the runaway climate train. Paul Hawken's very helpful book, *Drawdown,* is a great way to learn about options out there and to prime your pump for the important changes we all need to make.

You may have noticed a plea—to those of us who use more than our worldly share of resources—a plea to begin to contribute less to the carbon load in the atmosphere—a plea to the best of who you are, to use your inner moral compass to evaluate the rightness of your actions during this critical time on the planet. Your best nature is being summoned because only so much carbon can be allowed into a stable atmosphere, and because lower income countries and people *need* a certain amount of energy to progress. Actual people in other parts of the world— who live with less income and abilities to avoid the climate consequences—also desire health, safety and happiness.

We in the already developed world can manage our *wants* and we *can* scale back what we use. However, this is an especially challenging request for people in developing third world countries, who are simply trying to survive and gain a better and healthier standard of living. Our thoughtful response to this cruel dichotomy is to consider whether we *need* this item or trip. You may have perceived how *things* don't really make you happier.

Temporarily yes, but is the temporary blip worth it when you consider the rest of the world hinging on our choices?

Can we travel by other means?
Will our conferences be effective by phone?
Yes, because now technology allows us
to see each other while we speak.

These pivotal questions ask each person to consider the consequences down the road of ignoring the choices. The goal is for us all to survive and thrive. There is so much to do. Let's get started.

Preparedness is key. Bill McKibben is a hero, a climate activist, educator and author who looks to the future. He said on a radio interview, "One of the best things we can do to prepare for climate change is to live where there is a strong sense of community.... where there are people we know and can count on." This is how we once lived, in close-knit, often rural communities where contingency planning was part of life. Provision for unforeseen events was necessary because there were no backups. But today we love our conveniences and expect our devices and services to continue as expected—that is to be available exactly when we want them. Remember how frustrating it is when computer systems don't work and you lose the incredible abilities to connect with a world we have come to depend on? Imagine living in Puerto Rico, thrust into an electricity-less time for many hot and humid months. Imagine not being able, because you have no refrigeration, to receive the medications your life depends on. It challenges the imagination to be thrust back in time a few centuries, yet this is what Puerto Ricans lived for months. Listening to them tell about their lives after Hurricane Maria is a horrid wake-up call. The Caribbean Islands are a sure warning for us all. It is time to hear the call. We need to prepare.

A new genre of fiction labeled as "cli-fi" (climate fiction) envisions a potentially devastating future not unlike what Puerto Rico is going through, only, of course, on an even more dramatic scale. I'm not sure where I came across this quote from Cormac McCarthy, a cli-fi author, but it holds possibility. McCarthy thinks cli-fi has "the power to scare us into action and to wake us up while there is still time" ... or, he says "only fiction can frame events as teachable moments." You'd think the summer of 2017 brought enough teachable moments; still, if cli-fi is what it takes, great. I wish for this to work, yet right now it appears we need to be pushed and scared into action.

An erratically disrupted climate very well may kick us into gear for more comprehensive thinking and planning. I say 'may' because many people may go back to life as usual until the next disaster hits them personally. Even so, preparedness and a long-term view are essential for the rest of us as we plan for contingencies in light of these changing times. If the events of 2017 turn out to motivate significant numbers of people, then their towns, cities and states will need to follow this momentum, and to prepare for what could be in store.

Planning ahead for the levels of the recent disasters involves so much of the unknowable. For certain though, locating the most heat-vulnerable elderly, disabled, or less literate people is a first order, for they will require swift assistance. Multiples deaths in a nursing home in Florida after Hurricane Irma destroyed power for air conditioning illustrate how devastating excessive heat can be. Preparedness allows towns to swiftly open emergency cooling centers for heat sensitive people nearby, and to alert power suppliers to boost electricity when temperatures reach unhealthy levels. Rural areas must plan for access to enough water and shelter. Accommodations must be made to adjust the schedules of outdoor workers. Heat is but one example; choose your disaster—flooding, excessive rains, snowfall, power lines down, whatever. Long-term thinking grants time to imagine the possibilities and to organizing for those events. These words invite you to move yourself forward into a time we trust will stay within the imagination.

I've written quite a lot about preparation, but before dipping deeply into that, let's step back a moment and really consider: What in the world are we doing? We are witnessing the results of overusing finite resources.

Finite means when used up, there are no more,
as in oxygen crowded out by a carbon-intensive atmosphere;
as in fish whose stocks have depleted;
as in no fish to eat;
as in 1000-year-old topsoil washed into the Mississippi River;
as in mineral-depleted soil left behind for growing healthy food.
Gone, all gone, and now what do we do?

Oops, we haven't had a breathing break in a while.
Time do that.
Breathe deeply into your belly—effortlessly and easily.
Think of something or someone you love.
Spend time in your imagination.
Feel relaxation spreading though you.

My response to the questions above was to create an *Earth Restoration Plan (ERP)* containing specific straightforward and ready-to-implement strategies—to think cooperatively—to restore, not only to escape or mitigate, but literally to regenerate what has been rent. Relearning how to work cooperatively is essential to changing how we live. Human history benefitted from working together, but our hyper-individualistic American ways muddle those ancient memories. It's in our genetic history—*we will want to remember how to work together* so the worthwhile advantages of cooperation live for us again.

ERP intends to show what each person can do now, by pitching in with the work and by telling friends and family about what they are doing. Looking for what appeals to you is the best approach to any endeavor. Find what attracts you and get going right there. Then look for other pieces with new ideas that jump out at you— and tell others. This is sort of like playing the telephone game— with a major difference—here the last person hears the meaning and driving force of the original conversation and expands upon it. ERP is a simple enough invitation for everyone to join in with the challenge and the enjoyment. I say "enjoyment" because consciously choosing to do something meaningful feels really good.

Both the Earth Restoration Plan, Citizens for a Cooler Rhode Island, and The Climate Mobilization basically serve to preserve our human place on the earth. No small order! ERP is designed to educate, invite, urge and to call on people's best natures to join in—soon, for the need is great. Engaging people in what is possible NOW is a most meaningful first step, rather than passively waiting and watching the clock tick while governments debate. Calling on well-known people is how we create a louder voice and a broader audience. What these prominent people say will convey the urgency along with the crucial aspects of what each of us can do. The call from respected leaders in all fields will alert organizations and funders to use their momentum to speed the process of enormous climate action.

The more the merrier in all ways—everyone is required for such a massive project. This means you and you and you are being summoned. You will be surprised where your first step brings you, and you will be surprised when you discover ideas you didn't know about. The second, third, and fourth steps you take will build a progression into cooperation. And then along comes the next best brightest idea. You may feel good about this new path, so the next chapter will show you even more specifics about getting started.

One who is mostly an observer thrives in good times
but suffers in bad times...
(The reason is) ... the Universe accepts ...
(his point of view) and gives him more of it.
So the better it gets the better it gets.
Or the worse it gets, the worse it gets.
While one who is a visionary thrives in all times.
—Abraham Hicks

This means you and you and you are being summoned.

CHAPTER 10
Getting Specific

Accepting the science of climate change
yet doing nothing is immoral.
Our goal is not to amass information or to satisfy curiosity,
but rather to become painfully aware,
to dare to turn what is happening to the world
into our own personal suffering and thus to
discover what each of us can do about it.
Feel the pain of climate truth, and let it change you;
let it guide you towards engagement.
Accepting climate truth can affect
not only your civic and political engagement,
but also your priorities, goals, and sense of identity.
—Pope Francis

Prioritizing climate change and clean energy into our lives seriously matters. The Earth Restoration Plan below is a good place for individuals to begin. As momentum builds, people in communities can join together to demand that towns create some of the proposals. There is a lot here, so hold your breath and jump in. Find the changes that inspire you and begin there.

- State programs are available to retrofit homes and businesses. Use them. Simple and sensible insulation, tight windows and caulking are perhaps the most impactful and least expensive ways for homeowners to save energy and decrease carbon in the atmosphere. Everyone can help. These simple measures create jobs in communities where you live and they are a first move toward home efficiency. If you can afford to take further necessary steps, please do.

- Here are notable products to investigate, buy and use: (See the Resources and checklist sections at the end of the book)

- Renewable large-scale home batteries store energy gains from wind and solar. Efficient battery storage makes renewable, non-fossil fuel energy available at night and on cloudy days. The Tesla Powerwall is the most well-known storage unit to date. For sure, more varieties are coming.

- Solar generators are obtainable and handy for when storms knock out the power. These generators are quiet, don't turn your neighborhood into the earth shattering sounds of hell, nor do they use fossil fuels.

- Solar installers, equipment and financing programs are readily available.

- Small and more affordable, non-intrusive and concentric rooftop windmills are being produced in Europe.

- Heat pumps save energy, carbon emissions and money for heating and for air conditioning homes or offices. Homeowners report 50% energy reductions, cost savings and speedy installation.

- Efficient hot water heaters use less energy. Tankless hot water heaters are one example. Maintaining gallons of hot water at constant temperatures makes no sense as it wastes non-renewable sources of energy.

- At the very least, turning down the hot water thermostat saves energy (and money).

- The Energy Star program is a guide to more efficient appliances, which then save electricity.

- Induction electric cooking stoves are high efficiency and comparable to cooking with gas.

- Low moisture, front loading washing machines are more efficient.

- Perhaps a smaller refrigerator will suffice—massive is no longer ideal.

- How we transport ourselves is a massive sphere to interrupt. We truly must change how we get around, and surprisingly, the change can be pleasant.

- Carpool or use mass transit.

- Driving many miles per day with non-renewable gasoline emits carbon and harms the environment. Some 20% of car trips in the U.S. are less than a mile. Walking this mile instead of driving cuts emissions and gives you moderate aerobic activity. You could bicycle even farther and save your carbon input.

- Seeing is believing. Calculate the amounts of carbon produced by the miles you drive each day: *shrinkthatfootprint.com/calculate-your-driving-emissions*

- Buy electric, hybrid or enhanced miles-per-gallon cars if possible.

- Eat less meat.

  - Analysis shows that livestock and their byproducts account for at least 15% of annual worldwide emissions. GHG.[85]

  - Cutting back on the meat you eat saves money and makes each of us part of the change we need to be.

---

[85] Goodland and Anhang, "Livestock and Climate Change," *World Bank/IFC Report*, 2009.

- Ask yourself, can I do any better? Might I eat a little less, maybe cut back just a little at a time as I learn how healthy and satisfying less meat can be?

- Check your travel urges. The aviation industry uses 11% of transportation-related emissions in U.S. One single flight equals 20% of an average car emissions per year.

  - Educate and persuade yourself to travel less by airplane.

  - If you are an academic, politician, or business person, consider the long-term consequences of your many flights to conferences.

  - Reflect on the actual *needs* to be at that conference or to take as many trips.

  - If you have huge boats or many houses, or are a "snowbird" who flees winter, consider your choices.

  - If you are a frequent traveler, simply notice the numbers of times you travel by plane and reflect on how else you can be present and informed.

  - Choose to be smart with your choices.

  - Calculate the carbon footprint of your travels at *https://calculator.carbonfootprint.com/calculator*

- Choose more fuel-efficient airlines. Flying coach is more efficient.

- Nonstop airlines save fuel.

- Buy carbon offsets when you fly, and most of all … fly less.

- Purchase a carbon offset certificate. This strategy mitigates the impact of your emissions with investments in green projects, forests, renewable energy projects, or methane capture to reduce carbon in the atmosphere. Research for the best products. Shrink your footprint first before you buy offsets.

Now is the time to rethink the commonplace and to weigh your choices.

Begin your game plan for making change by reflecting on how you use and misuse energy (we all do), before you strategize to lower your personal energy uses. Consider whether you can make different everyday choices. The essential nugget is to make the reasons for your choice really important to you. You will most likely do what is truly important. Make a detailed plan to include both learning about and giving thought to the tools you need. Make understandable and measurable goals, along with timetables. This degree of specificity stirs a power to bring about meaningful change. With your big plan in mind, let's drill down even further to basically rewire old habits.

- Turn out the lights when you leave a room. No light on equals no electricity used. Turn down the heat when you leave the room or house.

- Investigate putting zones into your heating system.

- Turn off computers and printers at the end of the day.

- Place someone in charge of turning equipment on to be ready for office workers in the morning.

- Share your car.

- Keep tires inflated.

- Wear warm sweaters rather than turning up fossil fuel heat. Sweaters are passive heaters. Cats too.

- Reuse, reuse and reuse: bring cloth bags when you shop. This becomes a habit. Broccoli and avocados fit nicely into a cloth bag, while you reserve the plastic bag for the 4,000 peas you buy.

- Reuse plastic bags for garbage, for picking up dog poop, what else?

- How can you reuse your clothing? Lieberman, McLeish and Pippa report in their article, *Life Better*, that across the globe some "25 pounds of textiles are produced per person—in the U.S., more like 100 pounds each."[86] The authors also consider much of what we buy as not recyclable because it is an inexpensive mixture of cotton and polyester, which does not degrade in a landfill.

- Look at what you throw away. Can it be recycled or given away?

- Engage your family in a game to consider every action and figure out ways to do more with less.

- Food waste contributes nearly as many emissions as road transportation.

    - Reduce your waste.

    - Compost your leftover vegetable waste and make great soil for the spring. It's simple - just put your vegetable waste in a pail, save it inside and then take it out to a big bin so it can turn into fine growing soil.

    - Consider your choices about your family's size.

---

[86] Ellen Lieberman, Todd McLeish, and Jack Pippa, "Life Better," *University of Rhode Island Quadrangles Magazine,* Winter 2017.

- Non-polluting renewables save money in the long run—to where looking at heating bills becomes exciting.

This is a lot of information to take in, so please take your time with it. Review the list over and over until these actions become commonplace for you.

The goal in all of the efforts is to reach a tipping point number where people contribute their best attempts at turning around the ship of climate change.

- Talk to everyone about all of this. Climate change has been sort of a no-go zone - too heavy, no hope, let's talk about something fun.

- Make climate change a positive topic of conversation. We have to make it feasible to talk about. We're good at talking; so let more and more people understand the gravity of where we are and especially what we can do. We've looked at ways to begin by sharing some of the positive stories of what is already begin done. We've talked about asking people what they notice in their own lives. Tell them how inspired you feel about what you are doing to contribute to positive change. We have tools now for turning around pessimists. Talk about possibilities when you do begin and about the risks of not joining in.

Together we can do much to slow and even turn around the progression of negative effects. The Earth Restoration Plan and Citizens for A Cooler Rhode Island intend to build momentum to a stage where state governments adopt and promote plans to encourage responsible proactive behaviors in residents. By educating as many folks as possible, we will jumpstart the process and motivate early adopters, funders, celebrities and investors to both reduce their own carbon inputs and to inspire others to do the same. These well thought out plans from CACRI and ERP can spur on many of us long before national politicians sort out ways to begin lowering carbon emissions. The goal is for substantive, rapid and decisive actions to encourage others to take them up and change how they go about their lives.

Once you are settled into changing your own habits and behaviors, it is important to reach out to people and governments in the communities where you live. There are strategies to help with this, but first it seems useful to come up with a compelling positive and simple statement to document the urgency and to invite, encourage, and call upon each person's devotion to country and community, their commitment to world order, and their generosity to their grandchildren, to call on their goodwill. You may want to write your statement and make it into an elevator speech to help you get started.

Make it short and sweet—as in—
I am excited to be part of a very positive program
having good results.
What I do affects the earth.
After discovering how my actions
are part of why climate change is happening,
I don't want that role any more.
I'm learning to pay attention now.
It feels really good to question my actions
to stand for climate health,
to protect a safe, healthy community and country
for my children and grandchildren.
To learn simple ways to help our country and earth.
Will you join me in learning?

A strong statement opens the door to approaching communities for more substantive action. You can:

•   Form community, neighborhood, home and business energy grids to combine solar cost benefits for the community, to save money by buying equipment and by selling solar produced energy. Less transmission distances from combined installations benefit the earth and make more energy available. Again, less carbon emissions.

- Ask your marketing whiz friends to help spread this plan for an overall project to promote available solar incentives and newly developing technologies.

- Ask local government to create a database where people can research emerging renewable processes and available technology they can use.

- Ask your local government to encourage that solar panels be voluntarily installed on all commercial and educational flat rooftops. As momentum builds, governments can instigate further compliance. Abundant space on rooftops over our heads need not go wanting when solar panels can produce clean renewable energy and drastically reduce carbon emissions.

Andrew Winston, visionary author of *The Big Pivot*,[87] calls on businesses to think and to act differently—now, not later. He says the weakened "foundations of our planetary infrastructure are costing businesses dearly and putting society at risk. The mega challenges of climate change, scarcity, and radical transparency threaten our ability to run an expanding global economy and are profoundly changing business as usual." The language of economics resonates with our culture. Delay in the realm of climate change is bad for business. Theoretically, a healthy economy helps us all. The bottom line is, we have reached an economic tipping point and businesses must alter their practices. The good news is: low or no carbon, climate-resilient business practices offer enormous opportunities. Those companies which are already

---

[87] Andrew Winston, *The Big Pivot* (Harvard Business Review Press, 2014)

climate proactive have a head start. By now they have found plenty of resources to make themselves more efficient and to produce less carbon. Protecting their businesses with this standard of cost effectiveness places them ahead of their competition. Such a clear-eyed mindset makes a practical and compelling case in light of potential threats.

Pedram Shojai, filmmaker and a concerned businessman, rounds out this chapter with emphatic words from his "Prosperity":

"Get off the sidelines and join
the biggest opportunities of your lifetime.
We're literally BOMBARDED by information
telling us there's nothing we can do.
Might as well sit at home and just take whatever comes
because you don't individually have the power
to make real changes.

The problem is... that's 100% B.S.

Seriously SNAP OUT OF IT
That kind of energy won't help the problem,
and frankly it drags everyone else down.
It's absolutely the opposite of the energy
we're going to need to do our part.[88]

Pedram continues to say in the film, "No matter how small, or how insignificant you might THINK your actions are – I challenge you to get up and do something, ANYTHING positive and be a part of the

---

[88] Pedram Shojai. "Prosperity"

solution. Fatalism and the idea that we're helpless is a spiritual malady of our modern times. YOU can cure it by doing good things on your own for others to see."

Uplifting ourselves and those around us brings us out of the depression and hopeless feelings of not being able to do anything. "It's too big, too hard, too impossible"—all suggestions which lead up to the thoughts—"why not just give up and have fun?" Why not take drugs, drink, shop, watch television, incessantly look at Twitter and Facebook and be depressed? A spiritual malady indeed. Get up and do something!

From a recent conversation,
"Oh you always cared about the environment;
so that's why you're so involved."
Yes, I have—because—
We are the environment.
We depend on it and unless we realize our connection,
we may lose our way home.
Without a healthy earth, we are toast.
Whether the name is environmentalist, climatist or earth realist,
it's imperative we leave off the separation
and know ourselves as part of the whole.
We are earth and earth is us.

CHAPTER 11
Personal Story

♪♪ I'm driving on sunshine... and don't it feel good!!![89] *♪♪*
♪ ♫ ♪

My story comes out of many years of making our homes more sustainable. In one way and another all my efforts have been to protect and preserve the beauty and bounty of this earth, our mother. I have been a long-time organic vegetable and flower gardener, recycled, composted vegetable waste and been thrifty about using resources since the seventies. I co-founded a non-profit organization called Winter Green, whose mission was to help people recognize the opportunity to create a secure, local food source in the warm southern winters of Asheville, NC. And on and on...

I heard the call in the seventies to responsibly use the finite resources available to us all, and I never let this message go. Not that I'm a purist by any means, yet I try to use less and conserve

---

[89] "Walking on Sunshine" by Katrina & The Waves, 1983.

more. I bought *The Passive Solar House* by James Kachadorian and *The Solar Greenhouse Book* by James McCullagh and got to work studying. My husband and I built a solar greenhouse addition onto an old colonial house and also installed a wood stove. Years later we had our builder construct a new house oriented toward the south for passive solar gains. This house had passive solar rooms, a wood stove, energy-efficient triple-pane windows as well as plenty of the best rated energy-saving insulation in the thick walls and roof. Many years later I purchased a green-built home with thickset walls for energy conservation and with radiant floor heat. This house also had a southern orientation with south-facing windows for heat gain and boasted a rooftop solar hot water system. The warm radiant flooring was a pleasure to feel beneath my feet, and the heating bills were low.

Greening my very ordinarily built, inefficient home in Rhode Island is the latest in my string of efforts to minimize my carbon footprint. A state energy audit began the process by first sealing leaky spaces to keep out cold air. The workers then added extra ceiling insulation and installed new energy-saving lightbulbs everywhere. They answered my questions and left information about what else could be done. This first not-so-glamorous step was simple and effective in lowering heating and cooling costs. These steps also lowered my carbon emissions. A win-win.

Burning oil for heat has always bothered me. This just seems wasteful. Oil is a non-renewable resource which requires great amounts of energy to discover, pump from the ground, refine and then transport long distances. To top all that off, transporting oil and gas is hazardous. So many oil spills happen and trains explode. Gas lines regularly leak methane, a lot of it—in point of fact—more than cows give out. (Remember, cows are a major emitter.) We often don't hear about all these complications, and when we do it is shocking—as it was recently when refineries unleashed toxic chemicals on unsuspecting neighborhoods in Houston after the hurricane. Some people pay a very big price for our collective use of oil and gas. Every step of the way from ancient dinosaur residues deep within the earth to refined products heating our homes is a dangerous and polluting business. I wanted as little part of it as possible.

The first step I took to use less oil in my Rhode Island home was to install a super-efficient wood stove, which keeps me cozy and releases very few particles into the air. After this addition I learned about other alternatives to reducing my oil usage. Cold climate Mitsubishi heat pumps make for efficient heating and for my rare use of air conditioning. The units save around 50% of my heating costs. Because heat pumps function best above 20°, the wood stove takes the edge off when the cold air outside drops into the teens and single digits. Backup systems are necessary in the Northeast, and my oil furnace downstairs performs this service occasionally. The switch to electric heat by way of heat pumps was not a totally green solution. It is a better long-term option because eventually electric companies will incorporate more and more renewable resources into their mix of fuels. This means they will use increasingly less oil and gas. Pressure from customers will drive this change and lower the costs of solar and wind as their use prevails with the electric companies.

Investigating solar panels for my roof, partially shaded by large oak leaves, was the next step in greening the house. The first company I spoke with said, "No, there were too many trees around." So I moped, and then discovered a solar aggregating company. This brilliant idea matches people who have solar panels with other people who want solar but live in shady or rented houses. The idea is that the shady people and the renters buy energy from the aggregating company while the sunny solar owners sell their collected energy to the company. I bought into this plan, and nonetheless still wanted my own solar panels, which would give me more energy. A couple of years later, the technology advanced enough that sunlit solar panels will still function when parts of the panel are shaded. Wahhh laaa! Another sparkling idea! I was excited and contracted SolarCity to install the panels with a leasing system, which makes solar panels very affordable and do-able. Besides, I love the enthusiasm each employee shows about working for a company doing good in the world. Their passion is making a difference.

Now my monthly summer electric bills of $0 are exciting to see. Especially rewarding is the zero-carbon released into the atmosphere. Of course, a bill of zero dollars changes as summer wanes, nonetheless my bills are significantly less than before. Each reduction in cost represents less oil used and less pollutants emitted. On top of all that, my car charges with electricity; so I drive on sunshine. I feel good about the whole change. I suspect it is important to be uplifted by your contribution to these times. It is for me.

Discovering how else I can save energy and lower carbon inputs has become a game for the pioneer in me.

1. I installed plexiglass inserts called *Indows* on some leaky windows. They keep air and noise out as they make a room warmer and save energy.

2. When my old kitchen stove stopped working well, I researched options and discovered *induction* stoves, which use much less electricity and are as pleasurable to cook with as a gas range. The burners heat up immediately when you turn them on and their heat stops straight away on turning them off. Needless to say, I love this stove and its efficiency.

3. My next step is to have my hot water production become more efficient.

4. Greening the house is important to me. Therefore, greening my interactions with the world is another valuable goal. To do so, I:

5. am in the process of learning to eat less meat. I eat a veggie meal two or three nights a week. A gradual transition accustoms me to new ways and fascinating recipes for meatless meals. What I cook now is intriguing, tastes good and I don't feel deprived.

How did we get caught up in this rat race
of thinking we need quite so much meat and dairy?
We don't, and it is interesting to change up a diet.

Continuing on, I:

6. often shop for clothing at consignment stores. This helps to decrease the numbers of unnecessary clothes shipped across the world. Not sure if this tiny amount is true, but every little bit helps. I try to walk my talk so my suggestions for others to consume less have more validity.

7. have always valued the outdoors. Simply being in nature restores my spirit. I get exercise with walking my dog, doing outside garden chores, hauling wood for the stove and shoveling snow. These forward-looking benefits leave me becoming fit enough to walk farther at a time when we may need to. That is my plan and I'm sticking to it.

8. hang my clothes out to dry on a line. A clothes drier is one of the most energy intensive users in the house. The benefits are many: fresh air, time to listen to the birds and to be part of nature.

9. don't shower and wash my hair every day because this is an excessive waste of heat, water and fossil fuels. Neither I nor those around me suffer for this decision.

An important part of shifting gears into a more sustainable way of life is to remember to care for yourself as well. My first book, *Claiming Space: Finding Stillness that Inspires Action* can lead you into ways to take care of and inspire yourself to meaningful endeavors.

My choices to live more in line with nature and her abilities to restore herself reward me. It's a work in progress, as I still use plenty of fossil fuels; nonetheless I continue to evolve. I engage in a trying out practice for when it becomes necessary to do even more. These steps will, in time, become *necessary*, in the undoing of our 'progress is our most important product' attitude. The overall scheme behind my madness is to figure out what I can do, what can be done easily. Then, by sharing these ideas, other people can be part of the climate revolution.

I felt compelled to write this book to share with you that positive forward movement is stimulating. It feels good to be part of something constructive, as the enthusiastic solar installers recognized. Witnessing without this level of action and participating in the consequences of eons of human behaviors and actions is truly discouraging. Why not turn this sad state around and look for the phenomenal best of what we humans can be?

CHAPTER 12
Making *Common Sense* of it All

A Second Notice

15,364 scientists from 184 countries on November 13, 2017
published an open letter warning humanity
for the second time
against catastrophic biodiversity loss
and widespread misery for humans.
Their cautionary message implored humans
to make major changes.

That is, for people to cut greenhouse gas emissions,
phase out fossil fuels,
reduce deforestation, and to reverse the trend
of collapsing biodiversity.
Soon, science says, it will be too late to shift the course away
from our failing trajectory, and time is running out.
We must recognize, in our day-to-day lives
and in our governing institutions,
that Earth with all its life is our only home.[90]
—Sydney Pereira
Newsweek Magazine

---

[90] Sydney Pereira, "How to Save Humanity: 15,000 Scientists Urge Action Before 'Vast Human Misery' Takes Over," .*Newsweek*, November 13, 2017.

The scale of changes and the severely short time frame in which to turn the planetary ship around is absolutely true. And yet, this need not freeze us in place forever. The way out of fixation is to take constructive part in doing what we can. Acting rather than stewing feels good. Talking with others about what we are doing and why we do so empowers us toward the many actions required. We can do this.

The name *Climate Sense: A Practical Guide to Finding Solutions and Keeping Your Cool* was chosen for a reason. Please take the time to reflect on the stark warning you just read. What does this mean as you feel your way into the words?

Of course, you will form your own conclusions in regard to our collective trajectory. You may have questions. Great. What do you want to know and where can you search for answers? You've read many resources for beginning your investigations. Once the responses are in hand, what will inspire you to action? Great. Go for it. What happens if you say no to all you have learned? Probably nothing right away, for the rolling effects of climate change will, for a while, take time to happen and more time for you to fully absorb. Take your time to grasp the consequences— you can revisit your choices.

The task as I see it is for each person to challenge herself to begin to take personal and collective steps to rearrange much of what he or she does. This is a learning process. The overriding charge is asking each of us to become conscious of the results of our actions over time. So much of what we do are habits of which we aren't even aware. We just do them, yet *each action has consequences*. We who live in relative freedom have great opportunity to examine closely the repercussions made on this earth. Residents in the U.S. do not have to duck bombs, and plenty of us have food on our tables and roofs over our heads. This degree of security gives us pause to become more aware of how we are living our lives.

We can change our habits and behaviors. What do I mean? It's easy to begin. Turn the lights off in a room when you leave it. Dress according to the seasons and use less heat or air conditioning. Hold onto your clothes long enough to wear them out, then replace them. Bring a coffee cup to your coffee shop. Ask them not to give you a straw or a lid if you use their cups. Explain why. Use bags other than plastic or paper. You can select from so many styles of bags to carry your goods. Chose how you get around. Walk more. Ride bikes. Share tools with your neighbors, etc, etc. as covered in depth in chapters 9 and 10. See Earth Restoration Plan on page 179. Do these things for a month and you will have entered the realm of new habits.

Imagine if you belonged to a family of four people. Maybe you do. Your imaginary family has a television in each bedroom, one in the tv room, one in the kitchen, and one in the recreation room, many of them turned on all the time. This same family has laptops for everyone, not to mention smart phones. And how many fashionable new clothes do they purchase each season? Do they eat meat at every meal and order out lots? Do they eat foods someone else prepared many nights a week? Do they have huge cars to get around in? Do they take frequent holiday and summer vacations where they fly to faraway places? Do each of these family members replace their cell phones for the next best shiny new gadget even when those they currently own work quite well? Do they carry around the ubiquitous plastic water bottle? Such scenarios are not far-fetched these days in an average American family. Do you see any room for changes?

These images may sound familiar to you. However, take a look at the energy embodied in each choice—*and they are choices*. Simply looking at this list, can you see areas where this family can bring their behaviors and habits more in line with using less energy and emitting less carbon? There are many ways to decrease carbon inputs and still improve the family's wellbeing. Home cooked meals are healthier and don't come wrapped in plastics made of hydrocarbon chemical inputs. Less electronic use brings families together. People can put down their cell phones and get off the computer. The family you imagined might even inspire their children by talking about why they are making new choices. Play with these scenarios and see what you come up with. Does any of it fit for you? There you go—a good beginning right away.

Signs of 'progress' fill neighborhoods everywhere with their large houses filled with many bedrooms. More and more is what we seek in the valueless world which urges us to throw away and get a new one of whatever we crave in the moment. Hurry, hurry, hurry, waste more. And then the trash we throw away washes ashore to cover once sandy beaches on faraway islands and riverbanks. Much of what we no longer like ends up as flotsam in the oceans before it lands in the guts of sea animals or before it traps them in its webbing. This waste requires energy to produce it in the first place and then energy to dispose of and to transport its sad tossed out plastic self to bulging landfills. Is this the best we can do?

Many Americans have become stuck in a lifestyle seriously out of relationship with the rest of the world. We don't often see trash-filled beaches or riversides. They are far away. We don't often hear about animals stuck in webbing or dying because they have ingested plastic bits. You must live near the seas to learn about this horror. It is common for us all to do what we do in relation to those nearest to us. Then we close out all else, no matter the background thrum of warnings that all is not well.

All is not well, and even if we are not aware of this warning, it has a present effect on us all. The dire forecasts have become background to everyday life. Why do you suppose so many people take anti-depressant medications or use great amounts of alcohol and recreational drugs? Of course there are many reasons, but might these substances serve to normalize ourselves to a world careening to a collision?

We in the wealthier world can get along just fine with less. *My point is to look at and then think about what you do and what you use,* especially as you imagine the combined results of millions of other people making similar choices. What you and they do becomes a major influence on the earth's life support systems. If the examples presented are a fair picture of you, might you reconsider some of it? More conscious vacation time activities and less carbon intensive automobiles benefit us all. Even eating slightly less meat means less carbon particles filter into the air. There are so many ways to make a difference and to help us all.

The way to stop this CC Lines ocean liner coming directly at us is for many, many, many of us to get busy. Learn what you can, talk to everyone, and let your conversations be optimistic and filled with what you learn and what you are doing. Together we are many. Together we are enormously influential. Do what you can to allow your life to take away less from the planet. Think through ways to afford to do more. Each of us can do something. Have a free energy audit, insulate more, buy those solar panels, lease that electric car, buy that big battery to charge your car and home. Stretch and do what you can. Put on your thinking caps and solve problems. Spread the word with enthusiasm and feel yourself become fired up with what you are doing and with what is possible together.

This is our best way forward. We don't need foot dragging leaders. We need our wholehearted selves! Let James Altucher's words as an entrepreneur and author prime your pump about creative thinking:

"We are constantly in a state of reinvention.
We have to be. You can't step in the same river twice.
That's why 'repeat' is important.
You only have to work on the daydream for a tiny bit each day.
That's all it takes. 1% per day compounds to 3800% per year.
Working on making a day dream come true, even a tiny bit,
makes me feel like my hands were put to good use today."

After reading this far about reasons for paying attention and about your potential actions, you may want to sit down with your family or just by yourself and take a little survey of what you do now and what you can do differently to become part of this movement toward living sustainably.

Perhaps this all sounds overwhelming and impossible; yet it is not out of the question. Re-read what James just said. *We begin with small steps-1% per day, which encourage us and motivate others to do the same.* We stand up and be counted. We stand up for government, corporations and for the wealthy to do more. For more is crucially needed.

There you have it.
The world is in your hands.
Simply begin.
Use your common sense and take just one small step.
And the world will thank you.

BIBLIOGRAPHY

"A climate in crisis," *Oxfam,* April 27, 2017.

Akkoc, Raziye. "Mapped: How the Migration Crisis is a Strain on Europe's Democracies," *The Telegraph,* January 21, 2016.

Anderson, Kevin, Professor of Energy and Climate Change, University of Manchester and Deputy Director, Tyndall Centre for Climate Change Research. Gordon Goodman Memorial Lecture, Stockholm, Sweden, September 26, 2017.

Banerjee, Song and Hasemyer. "Exxon, The Road Not Taken," *Inside Climate News*, August 16, 2015.

"Bangladesh: Floods and Landslides," *ReliefWeb,* June 2017.

Berry, Thomas, priest, leading cultural historian, ecotheologian and author of *The New Story,* Teilhard Studies, no. 1., 1978.

Chandler, David. "Kerry Emanuel: This year's hurricanes are a taste of the future," *MIT News,* September 21, 2017.

Claverie, Jean-Michel. Information Genomique et Structurale.

Civic Alliance for a Cooler Rhode Island. CACRI.org

"Climate change could kill 50-80% of Pacific fish species: A conversation with Rebecca Asch," *RadioNZ*, November 22, 2017.

"Climate Driven Migration in Africa," *European Council on Foreign Relations,* December 20, 2017.

TheClimateMobilization.org.

Connellan, Shannon. "Elon Musk had 100 days to build the world's biggest battery. He's done." *Mashable.com,* November 22, 2017.

Cooperative Institute for Research in Environmental Sciences (CIRES): Air Quality Study in Utah, February 18, 2012.

Corum, Jonathan. "Sharp Increase In 'Sunny Day' Flooding," *New York Times*, September 3, 2016.

Dovey, Rachel. "12 Cities Plan for Emissions-Free Neighborhoods," *Next City*, October 23, 2017.

"Encroaching Tides in Miami-Dade County, Florida," *Union of Concerned Scientists Magazine Fact Sheet,* 2016.

www.FootprintNetwork.org.

Ghosh, Amitav. *The Great Derangement*: *Climate Change and the Unthinkable*. Chicago: University of Chicago Press, 2016.

Goodland and Anhang, "Livestock and Climate Change," *World Bank/IFC Report,* 2009.

Gilding, Paul. *The Great Disruption.* London: Bloomsbury Publishing, 2011.

Hall, Shannon. "Exxon Knew About Climate Change Almost 40 Years Ago," *Scientific American*, October 26, 2015.

Harvey, Chelsea. "Should the Social Cost of Carbon Be Higher?" *Scientific American,* November 22, 2017.

Hawkins, Paul. *Drawdown: The Most Comprehensive Book on Climate Change*. New York: Penguin Books, 2017.

Hinkley, Patricia. *Claiming Space/Finding Stillness that Inspires Action*. My FiveStreams, 2014.

Johnson, Scott. "The Weight of Harvey's Floodwater Actually Made Houston Sink a Little," *Ars Technica*, September 6, 2017.

Johnston, Ian. "More than Seven Hundred Species Facing Extinction are Being Hit by Climate Change," *The Independent,* February 14, 2017.

Kalmus, Peter. "Community Choice Energy in L.A. Began with a Single Citizen," *YES! Magazine*, Fall 2017.

Kimmelman, Michael. "Mexico City, Parched and Sinking, Faces a Water Crisis. Climate Change is Threatening to Push a Crowded Capital Toward a Breaking Point," *New York Times*, February 17, 2017.

Klein, Alice. "Eight low-lying Pacific islands swallowed whole by rising seas," *New Scientist*, September 7, 2017.

The Lancet Countdown. October 2017. www.thelancet.com.

Lieberman, Ellen, Todd McLeigh, and Jack Pippa. "Life Better," University of Rhode Island *Quadrangles Magazine,* Winter 2017.

Levitt, Daniel. "With Increased Destruction, a New Tornado Alley Emerges," *Bloomberg,* August 8, 2017.

Lind, Dara. "The '500-year' Flood Explained: Why Houston was so Underprepared for Hurricane Harvey," *Vox Magazine*, August 28, 2017.

"Losing Ground," RI Coastal Resources Management Council, 2012.

"Love Canal Still Oozing Poison 35 Years Later," *New York Post*, November 2, 2013.

Martinko, Katherine. "Don't worry about perfection when it comes to zero waste," *Living/Green Home*, November 22, 2017.

McKibben, William. "Winning Slowly is the Same as Losing," *Rolling Stone Magazine*, December 1, 2017.

Meadows. Donnella. *The Limits to Growth*. Vermont: Chelsea Green Publishing, 2004.

Mignoni, Eileen. "Flooding is the New Normal in Miami," *Yale Climate Connections,* February 6, 2017.

Milman and Yuhas. "An American Tragedy: Why are Millions of Trees Dying?" *The Guardian*, September 19, 2017.

Nuwer, Rachel. "Rural Rwanda is Home to a Pioneering New Solar Power Idea," *BBC Future Now*, October 9, 2017.

Nature. https://www.nature.com/nclimate. September 22, 2017.

Nyman, Patti. "Methane vs. Carbon Dioxide: A Greenhouse Gas Showdown," OneGreenPlanet.com. September 30, 2014.

Oliver, Mary. *Blue Horses*. New York: Penguin Books, 2016.

100-Year Flood - USGS. https://water.usgs.gov/edu/100yearflood.html.

Pereira, Sydney. "How to Save Humanity: 15,000 Scientists Urge Action Before 'Vast Human Misery' Takes Over," *Newsweek*, November 13, 2017.

Pipher, Mary. *The Green Boat: Reviving Ourselves in Our Capsized Culture*. London: Penguin Books, 2013.

Pittman, Mark. "Chasing Methane: Years of Living Dangerously," *Public Broadcasting Service,* January 28, 2017.

Prado, Mark. "Marin Thinkers Join Effort to Tackle Sea-Level Rise," *Marin Independent Journal*, October 5, 2017.

"Residents, Cities Taking Charge of Protecting the Environment," Editorial Board, *Miami Herald* November 22, 2017.

Restuccia, Richard. "5 Causes of Drought," *JAIN Magazine*, August 16, 2016.

Rubinstein, Asimov, Lyons. "San Francisco hits 106 degrees— shatters all-time record," *SF Gate News*, September 2, 2017.

Salaman, Margaret Klein. "The Transformative Power of Climate Truth: Ecological Awakening in the Age of Trump," *The Climate Mobilization*.

Scher, Robin. "Why Plant Based Shrimp is the Next Veggie Burger," *Alternet*, October 18, 2017.

Shojai, Pedram. "Prosperity, an informational/motivational series," https://www.well.org.

Silk, Ezra. "The Climate Mobilization Victory Plan," TCM.org.

Tabary, Zoe. "Human frontiers: How much heat can the body and mind take?" *Thomson Reuters Foundation Newsletter*.

Tesla Powerwall. https://www.tesla.com/powerwall.

"Thinking in Systems: A Primer," *Sustainability Institute,* 2008.

Titley, David. "New Department of Defense Directive on Climate and Security," *The Center for Climate and Security*, January 20, 2016.

Titley, David. "The 2 degrees that matter most," The Conversation. *Salon*. August 30, 2017.

Torres, Noe. "Mexican Farmers Suffer Worst Drought in 70 Years," *Reuters,* November 25, 2011.

Tory, Sarah. "Religious communities are taking on climate change," *High Country News*, September 18, 2017.

"The True Cost of Carbon Pollution," Environmental Defense Fund.

Uhlenhuth, Karen. "Midwestern poultry farmers cut bills in half with new heating system," *Midwest Energy News*, October 12, 2017.

US Climate alliance & The Climate Group report. September 13, 2017.

"The US Military on the Front Lines of Rising Seas," *Union of Concerned Scientists*, 2016.

Vaidyanathan, Gayathri. "Methane Leaks from Oil and Gas Wells Now Top Polluters," *Scientific American,* April 16, 2015.

Vaughan, Adam. "Electric Car Owners Can Drive for Free by Letting Energy Firms Use Battery," *The Guardian,* October 2, 2017.

"Wildfires in West Have Gotten Bigger, More Frequent and Longer Since the 1980s," *The Conversation*, May 23, 2016.

Winston, Andrew. *The Big Pivot*. Boston: Harvard Business School Publishing, 2014.

ASSORTED RESOURCES

Information:
YaleClimateConnections.org—nonpartisan, multimedia service providing daily broadcast radio programming and original web-based reporting, commentary, and analysis on the issue of climate change.

Artists and Climate Change.com

CitizensClimateLobby.org—international grassroots environmental group that trains and supports volunteers to build relationships with their elected representatives in order to influence climate policy.

"Prosperity"—informational/motivational series of videos. https://www.well.org

SkepticalScience.com—Examines the *science* and arguments of global warming skepticism.

https://www.footprintnetwork.org—measures your impact on the earth in relation to how much nature we have.

Mulcahy, Diane *The Gig Economy: The Complete Guide to Getting Better Work, Taking More Time Off, and Financing the*

Life You Want. American Management Association. NY, NY. 2016. (I have not read this, but reviews describe it as a good resource)

Conscious successful companies:
ConsciousCapitalism.org - resource for businesses with a focus on purpose beyond profit alone.
JustCapital.com - ranks companies on the issues people care about.

Financial
Cornerstone Capital Group - CornerstoneCapinc.com—
Investment advisors for financial performance and positive social impact.

NewResourceBank.com—investors choose one of three impact areas to support with their deposits: clean energy projects, organic and natural products or nonprofit organizations.

Food
RodaleInstitute.org—organic farming research and information.

ThriveMarket.com—membership-based web-based retailer of natural and organic food products at reduced costs.

SeventhGeneration.com—source for plant-based products that are safe and that work well.

GrowWhereYouAre.farm—an inspiring group of people grow quality, local food in ways that support the ecology, encourage the economy and improve human health.

More than 200 meatless cookbooks are available at your local bookstores or online.

Green building
Global Building Council.org—promotes local green *building* actions and addresses *global* issues such as climate change to ensure that green buildings are a part of any comprehensive strategy to deliver carbon emission reductions.

Teracycle.com—a global leader in recycling hard-to-recycle materials.

Solar Energy Resources for Installers—cleanenergyauthority.com; SunPower, SolarCity, etc.

Equipment
Tesla PowerWall Charger- a battery backup for solar generation—Tesla.com

Compost pails can be bought nearby and online. Stainless steel is best.

Outside composting bins and instructions are available locally.

RISE—riseengineering.com. Rhode Islanders Saving Energy- an energy efficiency retrofitting program available in Rhode Island. Search for a similar organization in your area.

Solar Generators—Inergysolar.com, GoalZero.com, solargeneratorguide.com.

Reducing Carbon
https://carbonfootprint.com to calculate your impact on the earth.

Carbon Offsets—*nativeenergy.com; terrapass.com; carbonfootprint.com*

EARTH RESTORATION PLAN

Check off what you already do, and then search for what else you can do.

But first,

1. Learn more about climate change and its causes.
2. Notice what you are feeling as you consider the world's current trajectory—toward the end of civilization.
3. *Stay with the feelings and anguish of losing everything you know and love.*
4. What would you do to preserve what you love? Feel the deep emotions around this desire.
5. Imagine yourself taking constructive action and experience your feelings with this step.
    Your passion here is the engine to sustaining a better world. It will lead you on.

Now to begin:

No cost items.

*   Reflect on how you use and misuse energy (we all do in some ways.)
*   Ask for an audit from your state energy efficiency program.
*   Turn down the heat or air conditioning.
*   Wear warm clothes indoors in winter.

- Cool your house sufficiently in summer to be comfortable with lightweight clothing.
- Lower the heat when you leave the house.
- Use blinds to keep heat out.
- Lower your hot water temperature. 120° is sufficient.
- Streaming movies through a smart television uses only a few watts. (Game consoles use ten times more energy.)
- Laptops use less energy than desktop computers.
- Turn off computers at the end of the day.
- LED lights use 85% less energy, last 25 times longer and save money in the long run.
- Make a new habit to turn out lights when you leave a room. Teach your children to do so.
- Keep your refrigerator at 35-38° and 0° for the freezer.
- Unplug the old refrigerator in the garage when it's not needed.
- Eat less meat. You can teach yourself new and delicious recipes.
- Compost vegetable waste and use the results to make beautiful soil for your gardens.
- Use cloth bags when shopping. Make a new habit to remember them. *I can do this/you can do this!*
- Reuse plastic bags. They inevitably creep into our homes, so be creative before you recycle them.
- Buy fair trade and vintage items. Check how much you will wear the new clothes.
- Purchase fabrics thoughtfully. *Cotton and polyester mixes are not recyclable.*
- Consider how to reuse clothing.

- Donate old items.
- Hang clothes outside to dry. Enjoy the sunshine and birds while you are at it.
- Make climate change and what we can do a positive part of conversations.
- Find local climate action groups.
- Speak with Representatives.
- Vote to protect the environment.
- Walk and bicycle more to use your car less.
- Use *shrinkthatfootprint.com/calculate-your-driving-emissions*.
- Share your car.
- Keep tires inflated.
- Make a game with your family of how to use less of everything.

Low Cost actions
- Follow up with energy efficiency audit suggestions: insulate, caulk windows and doors.
- Look for incentives for tax credits and rebates to retrofit your house.
- When you need to replace your roof, install a cool roof with reflective materials to direct light away.
- Trees and shrubs planted around the home act as insulation.
- Energy efficient windows triple pane, doors and skylights.
- Look for the Energy Star label for greater efficiency when you buy appliances.
- Replace an old refrigerator for a more efficient one.

- Change to more efficient hot water systems which save you money.
- Carpool or take the bus or train.
- Buy carbon offsets.
- Join neighbors to form distributed energy grids.

Next step, more substantial investments for decreasing your carbon impact on the world (and saving money).

- Rooftop solar.
- Battery storage for solar gains.
- Heat pumps for heating and cooling save money.
- Electric, hybrid or high mileage car, which you share with others to get to work.
- Solar generator for when the main power sources fail.
- Rooftop windmills or geothermal heat sources.
- Low moisture, front loading washing machine.
- Install zones into your heating system.

ABOUT THE AUTHOR

In one way and another, most of my efforts have been to protect and preserve the beauty and bounty of this earth, our mother. I have been a long-time organic vegetable and flower gardener, recycled, composted vegetable waste and been thrifty about using resources. I co-founded a non-profit organization called Winter Green to help people recognize the opportunity to create a secure and local food source in the warm southern winters of Asheville, NC. And on and on...

My previous life as an artist often focused on nature, painting butterflies, woodlands, volcano, ocean. I built what I called 'Nature Nests' to bring the healing powers of nature to people confined indoors. The nests were comprised of several parts: hinged paintings of the ocean enclose a shallow wooden box filled with sand and shells. Taped sounds of the ocean and seagulls provide more sensory input to simulate being in a natural setting. Nature Nests proved restorative for patients in hospice, cancer settings and even in a psychiatric hospital.

Both nature and meditation provide the space for me to be still, reconnect with my own center and then discover my next steps. This perspective is worth sharing as a "Climate Concerns Counselor" in the fast paced, plugged-in culture of our lives these days. This background plus my medical education, holistic trainings and experience as an RN integrate into a comprehensive approach to what is unique within each person. I have received a BS and MA in Holistic Studies and Psychology, was licensed as an RN and undertook comprehensive trainings in Hakomi, Internal Family Systems and The Journey.

Pat lives near the ocean in Southern Rhode Island with her doodle dog and fluffy, gray cat.

Visit https://www.PatriciaHinkley.com to learn more.

Also by Patricia Hinkley

Claiming Space:
Finding Stillness that Inspires Action
looks at how to interrupt the information overload and stress
of everyday living and gain better control and happiness
over our lives.

———————

Chasing Sleep:
Lonely Tussles in the Dark
explores an alternative perspective to the sleeplessness
experienced by millions of Americans—not as a disease
to be fixed by traditional pharmaceutical methods
but by identifying and managing the stressors
that take us out of balance and resolving them.

www.ingramcontent.com/pod-product-compliance
Lightning Source LLC
Chambersburg PA
CBHW072138270326
41931CB00010B/1799